TOMBOY GIGI
AND THE FUGITIVE

Published by:
Achilles King Publishing
Los Angeles, CA 90016
darrylabarnes@yahoo.com

Packaging/Consulting
Professional Publishing House
1425 W. Manchester Ave. Ste B
Los Angeles, California 90047
323-750-3592
Email: professionalpublishinghouse@yahoo.com
www.professionalpublishinghouse.com

Cover Design and Interior Illustrations: TWA Solutions
First Printing February 2024
10 9 8 7 6 5 4 3 2

ISBN 979-8-9900685-0-6 (paperback)
ISBN 979-8-9900685-1-3 (ebook)

TOMBOY GIGI
AND THE FUGITIVE

A Novel

Darryl Barnes

PROLOGUE

On September 1, 2016, in Birmingham, Alabama, eighty-six-year-old GiGi was deep into a boxing match on her TV when the phone suddenly rang. She didn't care if God was calling; she didn't like being disturbed while watching her boxing matches.

The persistent ringing of the phone bothered Gigi to the point of spewing profanity as she walked over to answer it. Shouting into the phone, she demanded, "Who is it? What do you want?"

It was Gigi's daughter, Matilda Moore, on the other end.

"Mama, I know you're watching your boxing match right now, but I need a big favor. I have a very important meeting to go to at 2:30 p.m., and I need you to pick up Michael from school." Michael was Gigi's seven-year-old grandson.

Gigi, not pleased, replied to her daughter, "You are out of your damn mind. I don't miss boxing matches for anyone."

"Mama, please! I don't have anyone else to pick him up. He gets out of school at 3:20 p.m., and it's only fifteen minutes from your house."

"Tell me something I don't know; I'm just old, not senile." Gigi hung up the phone, cussing and fussing, and looking up at the clock—it was a quarter to three.

Then, as she heard "One, two, three" coming from her television, she muttered, "Damn," and swiftly walked back to watch the fight. She started shouting, "Get up, get up!" as the fighter she liked was knocked down. The referee began the count, reaching eight before the fighter was back on his feet. Gigi's applause followed, and she offered spirited guidance, saying, "Throw a left, no, not a right—throw a left uppercut!" Nevertheless, the fighter she was rooting for was knocked down once more. "I told you to throw a left and an uppercut; you don't listen. That's why you got knocked down again."

Gigi had a habit of speaking to the television as if the people on the screen could hear her. She glanced up at the clock, and it displayed 3:00.

She exclaimed, "I'm going to miss my fight! Where's my sweater? Let me go get this boy."

Upon arriving at the school, she noticed a group of boys harassing her grandson, Michael. They were tossing his books onto the street and had even pushed him down. Gigi abruptly slammed on her brakes, indifferent to the drivers behind her. As she stepped out of the car, the people in the cars behind her began shouting, "Are you crazy, old lady? What are you doing?" Unfazed, Gigi responded with a defiant gesture, raising her middle finger. She then popped the trunk of her car and retrieved a wooden bat. Determined, she marched across the street toward her grandson.

One boy who had been involved in the altercation with her grandson spotted her approaching with the bat and quickly alerted the others. They all scattered and ran away.

Gigi shouted after them, "What's up? Are you scared of an old lady with a bat?" She told her grandson Michael to get up from the ground and pick up his books. She then turned her attention to her grandson, Michael, urging him to get up from the ground and collect his scattered books.

In her frustration, she grabbed Michael by his ear, prompting him to cry out, "Why are you pulling my ear? That hurts!"

She sternly instructed, "Michael, get in the car." Despite the blaring car horns and people yelling at her, she remained resolute.

Once inside the car, Michael continued to hold his ear due to the pain. Tears streamed down his cheeks. Gigi glanced at him and remarked, "Are you crying? Boys don't cry." Michael didn't respond; he simply wiped his face in silence.

Upon returning home, Gigi turned the television on to see if she could catch some of the fight, but it had gone off. "Damn," she uttered and turned the TV off.

"I missed my fight because of you."

"I'm sorry, Grandmother."

Gigi responded sharply, "Don't call me 'grandmother'. You make me sound like an old woman. You can call me 'grandma'." Gigi then added, "Come with me; we are going to make a man out of you. No grandson of mine is going to grow up getting beat up."

Gigi had a backhouse that nobody had ever been in before; she kept it boarded up. As she led Michael toward the backhouse, she began recounting the story of what had happened to his father. "Your mom threw him back in the lake and went fishing again."

"My mom didn't throw my dad in no lake. He's on vacation."

Gigi couldn't contain her laughter, clutching her stomach, and then remarked, "One day, you'll understand."

"Give me that metal stick."

Michael asked, "What is this?"

"It's a crowbar." While Gigi was prying open the door, a mouse darted across her foot, startling Michael, who started screaming, "Grandma! Grandma, look, there's a mouse!" He took off running.

Gigi yelled out, "Come back here, boy!" Michael stopped running and started walking back. When he got back to the door, Gigi said, "I should take this crowbar and knock some sense into your head. Stop being afraid of every damn thing. That mouse is more scared of you than you are of it. Did you see it stop and say hello?"

"No, Grandma."

"Did you see it bite me?"

"No."

"You saw it run?"

"Yes," Michael said.

"Okay then, what's that telling you?"

Michael said, "It was afraid."

"Thank you. Now help me pull this door open."

After they opened the door, Michael covered his nose. "What is that stench, Grandma?"

"You'll get used to it. Come on in." She then switched on the light, and Michael entered, still holding his nose.

As Gigi pulled the sheet back from the couch, dust billowed into the air. She began wiping away the cobwebs and dust from the pictures on the wall. Michael walked over to the wall to look at the pictures. The first picture he saw was of a Black man in boxer shorts raising his fist. Curious, Michael asked, "Grandma, who is this colored man?"

Gigi didn't utter a word; she simply kept dusting off the pictures before she settled down on the couch.

Curious, Michael inquired, "Grandma, who is this little girl with this colored man?"

Gigi remained seated, her head down, not uttering a word.

Michael walked over to his grandmother. "Grandma, what's wrong?"

Gigi raised her head, tears streaming from her eyes.

"Grandma, why are you crying? What's wrong?"

Gigi brushed off her tears. "I'm not crying, boy; that's my allergies messing with me. That Black man you see in that picture is one reason I'm still here and why I love boxing so much. His name was Bo Henry Washington, the greatest street fighter that ever walked the streets, and that little white girl you see is me."

Michael returned to the pictures on the wall. "Grandma, is that really you?"

Gigi, sounding a bit defensive, retorted, "What you trying

to say, boy? Don't that look like me?"

"Yeah, Grandma, that looks like you."

Gigi then gestured for Michael to join her. "Now, come over here and sit down. I'm going to tell you how me and Bo Henry crossed paths. The year was 1908, July third, at 11:45 p.m., when Bo's mother's water broke."

"Grandma, how do you know when her water broke?"

"Bo told me. Now, shut up, and don't interrupt me again."

CHAPTER 1

Her name was Odessa Washington. She screamed out her husband's name, "John, get in here! It's that time." Odessa's two daughters, Mary and Melissa, came running into their mother's bedroom. Odessa yelled out, "Where is your father?"

Mary went running around the house, looking for her father. He had fallen asleep on the front porch. Odessa told Melissa to get a fire started for some water and to bring her all the rags she could find.

Odessa started screaming again. "He won't wait. Where the hell is your daddy?"

John came running in, saying, "Here I am, baby."

Odessa couldn't stop screaming. Mary and Melissa ran into the room with the hot water and rags.

Mary said, "Come on, Mama, push!" Mary was the oldest child, she was nine.

Melissa was wiping all the sweat from her mother's forehead. John was standing by her side, holding her hand.

Odessa screamed as loud as she could for the last time and the baby popped out. It was a boy. After Mary cleaned the baby up, Odessa told her to hand her baby boy to her.

Melissa said, "Mama, what are you going to name him?"

Odessa said, "His name will be Bo. Bo Henry Washington." Then, she looked at her husband. "Mr. John Lee Washington, take your son and hold him."

John took his son into his arms, then he walked outside on the front porch, looked up into the sky, and said, "Thank you, God, for a healthy baby boy."

As days turned into months and months turned into years, Bo was always getting into trouble. He couldn't control his temper and was always getting into fights. Bo's father tried over and over to talk to him about his temper, but it did no good. At the age of ten, in the year 1918, Bo took on a job after school as the water boy for Mr. Andrew Johnson, who was the greatest street fighter who ever walked the streets in the Deep South. Bo could not wait to get out of school. When he heard that school bell ring, all you could see was dust in the air. After making it to the barnyard where all the fights took place, it was so crowded with all the townspeople, Bo had to crawl on his knees to make it inside.

Bo heard the champ calling his name. Bo yelled out, "I'm right here, champ. In the middle of the seventh round, the champ was getting beat pretty badly. Bo started yelling, "Out left, left, your other left, uppercut! Yeah, that's it, champ."

The referee started counting to ten then he said, "Knockout!" and everybody jumped up cheering. After getting the champ into the locker room, they laid him down on this wooden table. The champ was hurt pretty badly. He was coughing up blood when a Caucasian man walked into the room.

He walked over to the table where the champ was and said, "Mr. Andrew Johnson." The champ opened his eyes and everybody backed away from the table. "My name is Tommy Moore from New York City, in case you didn't know. Mr. Andrew, your name is all over the place, forty-two wins and zero losses. I'll pay you $2,500 to come fight one fight in New York City. I know you don't make that kind of money down here in the deep South."

The champ said, "You're right, I don't. Who will I be fighting?"

"They call him Iron Fist Mike. He is also undefeated. Twenty-six wins and zero losses. I'll give you two months to get ready for the biggest fight of your life."

"What do I get after I win?"

Mr. Moore started laughing, and then said, "There isn't a colored boy on this earth that can beat Iron Fist Mike."

"We will see about that."

"Five thousand dollars is the whole package, but you won't win." Mr. Moore turned around and walked out of the room.

After a few hours of doctoring on the champ, they took him home. Bo had to stay and clean up the locker room before he went home.

While he was mopping up all the blood off of the floor, his father walked in and said, "Boy, it's about time for you to be getting home."

"Okay, Pa."

While Bo was still mopping, his father walked up behind him and said, "Son, I already see what direction you will be going in with your life. I've been watching you on the front porch at home, shadowboxing, and I know nothing I say will change your mind. You just remember one thing, boy. Education first! Without it, you won't make it in this world." Bo's father turned around and walked out of the locker room. Bo just stood there, holding that bloody mop in his hand, looking down at the floor.

The next morning, as Bo was walking out the front door, his father asked, "Boy, where are you going?"

Bo replied, "To school."

As Bo was walking down the dirt road from his house to go to school, his father looked up into the sky and said, "Thank you."

As time went on, Bo continued to go to school and work for the champ after school. Two months had come and gone. The whole town was cheering for the champ as he was about to depart and head for New York City. This had been the biggest thing that ever happened to this small town. Even the rednecks were cheering. Bo was pretty upset because he couldn't go, but the champ had told Bo, "I will see you in my corner coaching me on to victory. I wouldn't have won that last fight if it wasn't for you." That put a big smile on Bo's face.

One week later, every ear in town was glued to the radio. Bo couldn't sit still. He was talking shadowboxing like he was there in the champ's corner. The fight had gone to the fifteenth round, neither fighter had gone this distance before, and both were exhausted. Out of nowhere, the champ threw a right hook, knocking Iron Fist Mike down. This was the first time Iron Mike, the champion, had been knocked down. The referee started counting. Iron Fist Mike was trying to get up. The whole town of Juliet was counting with the referee. "Five, six, seven, eight, nine, ten! You're out!" The whole town went crazy. People started shooting guns in the air and blowing their car horns. You would have thought that it was the Fourth of July. A few days later, the champ returned home to a big celebration with Bo by his side.

After that big victory, the champ took a break from boxing.

Chapter 2

Years had come and gone. In 1926, Bo graduated from high school. His mom and pop were so proud of him. Bo's two sisters, Melissa and Mary, had moved on with their lives, both of them had married, and Melissa moved to California and Mary went to Florida.

Bo told his parents, "I don't plan on moving or getting married. I plan on being the future champ of this town."

After a few months, the champ was fighting a youngster from Dallas, Texas. They called him the Golden Boy. This kid was quick on his feet. The champ couldn't keep up with him. After the fourth round, Bo told the champ, "Stop chasing him. Let him come to you." The champ did what Bo told him to do, and in the middle of the seventh round, the champ knocked the Golden Boy out.

The champ's legs couldn't move like they used to back in the day. He knew his time was up. He couldn't walk to the locker room without Bo helping him. After getting the champ to the locker room, they found out that most of his ribs were damaged. That's why he was coughing up blood again. The champ knew that his days of boxing were over. He told everybody to leave the locker room except for Bo.

He said, "Kid, you've been in my corner since you were ten years old, and I have become the greatest because of you. I want you to cut these gloves off my hands."

Bo did what the champ asked.

The champ said, "Now, put them on your hands."

Bo put on the gloves, then asked the champ, "What now?"

The champ said, "It's your turn. Just remember, boy, there are three things that come with this territory: money, respect, and women. Don't let it get the best of you. Keep this little town alive."

A week later, on September 15, 1926, the champ passed away. It was the biggest funeral in Juliet, with Blacks and Whites standing side by side.

A year later, on October 4, 1927, the townspeople were cheering him on, "Bo, Bo, Bo!" It was Bo's first fight, and in the middle of the third round, Bo had knocked his opponent out. The crowd went crazy.

After the fight, Bo cleaned himself up and went to the club where everyone was waiting for him to arrive. It was a spot where colored people partied with a few white people who liked to join in the fun. Bo was on the dance floor, cutting a rug with two pretty ladies, when out of nowhere, a fine white girl pushed the two sisters aside and put her arms around Bo. She moved her body in real close as they danced. The two sisters stood there, rolling their eyes at the white girl, and then they walked off the dance floor, muttering under their breath.

Bo turned his head in the direction that the two sisters were walking, but the white girl took her hand and turned Bo's head back toward her. She said, "I'm right here; they're gone."

Bo loosened up his collar because he already knew that being seen with a white girl was trouble. "What's your name?"

"You can call me Sophia."

Bo and Sophia stayed on the dance floor for half of the night. After a few hours had come and gone, Sophia told Bo, "I'll see you later, champ," and gave him a kiss right on his lips.

After the club closed, Bo walked home. Since he was the town's champ now, he didn't have to live with his parents anymore; he had his own place a few blocks from the club.

When Bo got home and turned on the light, there was a big surprise waiting for him. Sophia was laying in his bed in her lingerie.

She said, "I told you I'd see you later."

Bo was taking off his hat, and Sophia turned off the light. After they began making love, Sophia started calling out the Lord's name, and the noise from the springs in that old mattress could be heard for miles.

Five miles across the railroad tracks, a lady named Betty went into labor, and she, too, was calling out the Lord's name. "Oh God! Oh God! Oh God!" She had gone into labor while she was at work at the corner coffee shop on Dean Street. She wasn't due for another two weeks, but the baby couldn't wait any longer. Everyone in the coffee shop did what they could, and there was no time to take her to the doctor.

The manager of the coffee shop yelled out, "We need two tables; get up and move!" All the dishes and food on the tables went flying onto the floor. He yelled out, "Bring me some tablecloths and a whole lot of rags." He told the cook to boil some water.

Diane, who was the other waitress, said, "I didn't know you knew how to deliver a baby."

The manager said, "I don't. This is what my wife yelled out when my daughter was born. Thank God my sister-in-law was at the house when her water broke."

Diane said, "Oh my God, what are we going to do? Does anybody in here know how to deliver a baby?"

Everybody said, "No!"

Betty was still calling out the Lord's name, and five miles across the tracks, Sophia was still calling out the Lord's name. Both ladies were saying it's coming at the same time.

Diane said, "Put her on the table; I'll be back."

The manager said, "Where the hell are you going?"

"I'm going to find Mimi."

Mimi was an old lady who had delivered half of the babies in town. Diane knew exactly where to find her, down the street at the bar. Mimi could drink a bull under the table, and the bar was just two blocks away. Diane jumped on a bicycle and headed to the bar. After getting there, she spotted Mimi at a corner table with a bottle of whiskey and a shot glass in her hand.

As Mimi put the glass to her lips, Diane snatched her out of the seat and threw Mimi across her shoulders. Mimi grabbed the bottle of whiskey off the table and yelled out, "Child, put me down! Where are you taking me?"

"To the coffee shop. Betty is having her baby."

Diane jumped on her bicycle and told Mimi to get on.

Mimi said, "Child, I'm not getting on no damn bike."

"I'll buy you a case of liquor after you deliver this baby."

"Move over, I'm driving."

After getting back to the coffee shop, the baby's head was already coming out. Betty was screaming at the top of her lungs. Mimi told everybody to move out of the way. She told Diane to hold Betty's legs and told the manager to hold her arms. Then she said, "Now push."

Betty was still screaming at the top of her lungs, and so was Sophia.

About twenty minutes later, Betty and Sophia had both stopped screaming.

Mimi yelled out, "It's a girl!"

Everyone in the coffee shop started cheering.

After cleaning the baby up, Mimi handed her to Betty.

Everyone was asking, "What are you going to name her?"

Betty said, "I'm going to name her Gigi."

As time moved on, Betty was still working at the coffee shop as a waitress. She would take Gigi with her to work every day. It seemed like people started coming from everywhere after Gigi was born in that coffee shop. The manager, Mr. Willard, didn't mind Betty bringing Gigi to work with her; he felt like Gigi was a good luck charm. He gave Gigi whatever she wanted.

CHAPTER 3

Five miles across the track, Bo was still knocking out every opponent that stepped in the ring with him. Before every fight, he would always look out into the audience until he spotted his main squeeze, Sophia. A lot of people in town knew about Bo and Sophia, but they still had to keep it on the down-low, especially since Sophia was the niece of George Thompson, the town's mayor.

Things slowed down for Bo since he was knocking out opponents left and right, and nobody wanted to fight him. He hadn't had a fight in the last three years. No one was interested in fighting him during this time. So, Mr. Angelo, the owner of the nightclub, gave Bo a job as a bouncer until someone was brave enough to get in the ring with him.

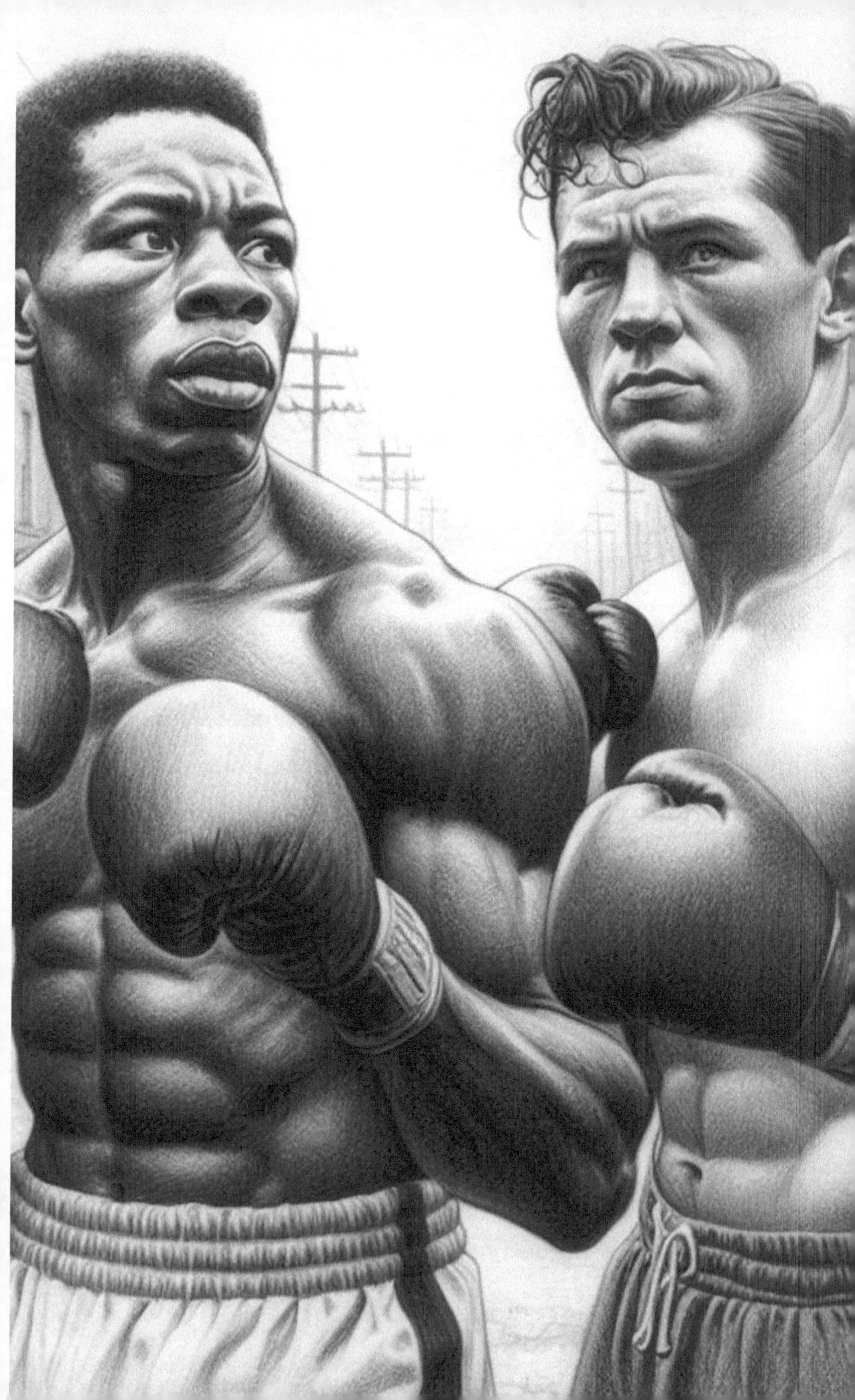

The majority of the time, when there was trouble in the club, Bo would be able to get things back in order with just a few words. But there's always one who will have too much to drink and think he's king of the jungle.

It was 11:00 p.m. Bo was standing by the front door, and the club was pretty crowded with people still coming in. Bo was greeting the people as they arrived when he heard someone say, "Get your hands off of me, man!" As Bo was walking through the crowd to see what was going on, he saw Gloria, one of the cocktail waitresses. Some man sitting at the table had his arm wrapped around her waist, telling her to bring him another bottle. The table was already covered with empty beer bottles. Gloria said, "Bo, get this man off me."

When the man saw Bo coming, he grabbed Gloria and forced her onto his lap.

Bo walked over to the table and said, "Sir, we don't want any trouble in here. Can you please let the waitress go? Or we're going to have to ask you to leave the club."

The man started laughing while he was downing another beer. Then he threw the beer bottle across the room. The bottle smashed against the wall, the music stopped playing, people stopped dancing, and it was quiet as a mouse. The man pushed Gloria out of his lap.

A lady walked up to Bo and whispered in his ear, then the man stood up. Come to find out, it was Big Country. He had just been released from prison, and he had been locked up for ten years for beating up twelve sheriff deputies.

Big Country was about six foot seven and he weighed about three-hundred-twenty pounds. When the people in the club saw Big Country stand up, everybody started leaving the club.

Big Country said to Bo, "What are you going to do, little man?" Then, he threw an uppercut, sending Bo flying across the room.

Bo came down on one of the tables, breaking it in half.

While Bo was trying to recuperate, Big Country ripped off his shirt and said, "Come on, little man, get up."

A few men in the club were helping Bo get back up on his feet. People started running back into the club. The word had spread throughout the town that Bo was fighting Big Country. People started coming from everywhere. Bo and Big Country were fighting in the middle of the floor in the nightclub.

Money was flying everywhere; some people were betting on Bo, and some people were betting on Big Country.

Bo knew he couldn't let Big Country get a hold of him, so he would punch and move at the same time. Big Country was throwing wild punches, and he was getting frustrated because he couldn't catch Bo with one punch. Bo couldn't reach Big Country's face, so he just worked the mid-section, the kidneys, liver, chest, and his shoulders. Big Country was getting tired; Bo knew he had him then. Big Country ran towards Bo, picked him up over his head, and threw him across the room. Bo went flying through the window, breaking the glass.

The fight was now outside, and people started turning on their car headlights. Most of the people were cheering for Bo, "Get up, Bo, get up."

As Big Country was walking out of the front door, he was throwing people out of his way, screaming, "Get up, little man! I ain't done with you yet."

Bo's right eye was cut pretty bad after getting thrown out of the window. Somebody in the crowd threw him a towel. Bo wiped his face off and said, "Come on, Big Country."

The crowd started screaming, "Yeah, get him, Bo."

Big Country started running towards Bo with his head down. Bo was able to move out of the way, and he grabbed Big Country by his overalls, smashing his head into a car headlight. The crowd started going crazy, and Big Country's face was all cut up from smashing into the car headlight.

While Big Country was down on his knees, Bo started throwing punches. Big Country threw a backhand, hitting

Bo right in his jaw. Bo went flying backward but was still on his feet. As Big Country turned around and stood up, there was this sound like it was an earthquake; it was Big Country's stomach.

Next thing you knew, everything in Big Country's stomach went flying everywhere out of his mouth. Everybody in the crowd got a taste of what was in Big Country's stomach. While Big Country was holding his stomach, he said, "I don't feel too good. I want my mama," then went face down to the ground. There was so much dust you couldn't even see Big Country. After the dust cleared, all you saw was a big hole in the ground.

The fight was over. Bo yelled out, "Get some rope, get him out of there, and take him home to his mama."

The crowd started cheering, holding Bo's arms up in the air. A few of the men picked Bo up and put him on their shoulders. They went back inside the club.

Big Country started snoring, so they just let him sleep it off.

Chapter 4

Five miles across the tracks that following Sunday morning, Gigi's mom, Betty, was knocked out sleeping on the couch with an empty bottle of whiskey laying on the floor. Gigi was trying to wake her mom up to let her know she was on her way to Sunday school. All her mom kept saying was, "Leave me alone, child, leave me alone," and waving her hand in the air. Betty was hungover from the bar she had gone to the night before.

As Gigi was leaving, she noticed a pair of boots sitting by the front door. She knew they weren't her mom's; she heard the toilet flush in the bathroom. She turned around, and there was a man she'd never seen before coming out of the bathroom. While fixing his pants, he looked up and saw Gigi, stopped right in his tracks, then he smiled and said,

"Howdy, little girl. Betty didn't tell me she had a daughter. What's your name?"

"My name is Gigi. What is your name, who are you, and what are you doing in our house?"

The man threw his hands in the air and said, "Slow down, soldier. Don't beat me up. My name is Bob. I'm a friend of your mom's."

Bob stuck his hand out for Gigi to shake, but Gigi just gave Bob a dirty look and walked out the front door.

While walking up the dirt road, Gigi's friend, Antoinette, was sitting on her front porch and saw Gigi coming up the road.

Antoinette said, "What took you so long? We're going to be late for Sunday school. Why do you have on those overalls? Didn't you wash out your Sunday dress?"

"I forgot."

"Well, come on in the house. You can put on one of mine. You can't go to Sunday school dressed like that."

"I'm seven years old now. I can wear what I want to wear."

Gigi didn't like wearing dresses, shoes, or socks. Half of the time she didn't even comb her hair. After walking a mile up the dirt road and across the railroad tracks, you could hear the church bells ringing.

"Come on, Gigi, run, or we're going to be late."

Gigi and Antoinette made it just in time as the doors were closing. This was Gigi's first time going to Sunday school, and she only went because Antoinette told her there would be a picnic after church. There was going to be a whole lot of food and candy.

After Sunday school was over, all the kids ran outside, getting ready for the picnic. Gigi felt a little out of place because she didn't know any of the other kids. Also, all the other kids had on clean clothes, shoes, and socks. Gigi and Antoinette were walking towards the tire swing, and a group of kids ran up behind Gigi and pushed her into the dirt. Antoinette backed up; she knew what was coming next.

One little boy said, "She can't get any dirtier than she already is," and all the kids started laughing.

Gigi got up off the ground, walked up to the little boy, and punched him right in his nose. The little boy hit the ground, holding his nose, crying.

Gigi said, "Who else wants some?"

All the other kids ran away.

Antoinette said to Gigi, "I'm going to teach you how to be a lady if it kills me. Girls don't punch boys in the nose."

"I do."

Antoinette just shook her head and grabbed Gigi's hand. "Come on, let's go eat."

None of the other kids messed with Gigi again.

While all the kids were playing and enjoying the picnic, Miss Johnson, the Sunday school teacher, called out for Gigi.

Antoinette walked over to where the boys were playing. "Gigi, Miss Johnson is calling you. Go and see what she wants."

Gigi replied, "I'll be back, don't start without me." All the boys had taken a liking to Gigi.

Antoinette said, "Look at you, your face is dirty. Dust your clothes off."

"What for? I'm just going to get back dirty again."

After getting inside the church, Miss Johnson said, "You two ladies come with me." They walked to the back of the church, where there was a big door with a lock on it. Miss Johnson took the lock off the door. "Ladies, come on in."

Miss Johnson pulled the string to turn on the light, and the girls saw a whole bunch of clothes, shoes, and hats. These were things that people in the town had donated to the church. Antoinette started jumping up and down, and Gigi's eyes got as wide as an owl.

Miss Johnson said, "Whatever you can carry, you can take home."

The girls got very excited because neither of them had many clothes at home. While looking through the clothes and shoes, Gigi saw an old baseball cap laying on the floor. She picked it up and dusted it off.

Antoinette said, "Gigi, girls don't wear no baseball caps."

Gigi replied, "This girl does," and then she put the cap on her head.

Miss Johnson started laughing, and Gigi and Antoinette said, "Thank you, Miss Johnson, for everything."

"You're welcome. Just make sure both of you are here next Sunday for Sunday school lessons."

"Don't worry, Miss Johnson, we will both be here, ain't that right, Gigi?"

I guess, but I'm not putting on no dress."

Miss Johnson covered her mouth while smiling and laughing. "That's fine. Wear what you want to wear as long as you come to Sunday school."

Gigi and Antoinette started walking home, and they both had big smiles on their faces. It was a long walk to Antoinette's house.

Gigi said, "See you tomorrow at school."

"Okay, Gigi, and wear a dress."

Gigi turned around, facing Antoinette, and stuck her tongue out at her. "You wear a damn dress!"

"Oooo, Gigi, did you just say a bad word to me?"

Gigi just stuck her chin in the air and kept walking down the dirt road.

After making it home, Butch, Gigi's dog, ran and jumped into her arms, knocking her on the ground. Butch was licking all over her face, and she started laughing and playing with her dog.

Gigi's mom, Betty, yelled out the window, "Gigi, where in the hell have you been? I've been looking for you all morning."

Gigi pushed the dog out of the way and got up off the ground. "I tried to tell you this morning that I was going to Sunday school with Antoinette, but you wouldn't wake up."

"Come get this note and take it down to the corner store. Tell Mr. Woods I'll have all his money by Friday."

"I don't need a note; I already know what you want. It's the same thing every day, cigarettes, and whiskey."

"Don't you get smart with me, little girl. You just do what I tell you to do."

"Why didn't you send that man to the store? He's been here all morning."

Gigi's mom ran from the bedroom window to the front door with a belt in her hand. Gigi took off running up the road; her mom ran to the front gate and said, "I'm going to get you, and don't you forget my damn cigarettes."

Betty's new friend was standing on the front porch with a cigarette in his mouth and a beer in his hand.

Betty said, "What am I going to do with this child?"

Her friend started laughing. "Just let the child be; kids will be kids."

Betty just shook her head. While walking back into the house, she snatched the cigarette out of Bob's mouth and the beer from his hand. "Just mind your business." She walked back into the house, puffing on the cigarette.

After Gigi and her dog, Butch, made it to the corner store, Gigi told Mr. Woods, the owner of the store, what her mom wanted.

Mr. Woods said, "Tell your mom this is the last time she can have credit until she pays what she owes me."

"Okay."

Mr. Woods handed Gigi a brown bag with two bottles of whiskey and two packs of cigarettes. Gigi and her dog started walking back home.

When they made it back to the house, Betty and Bob were sitting on the front porch.

Betty said to Gigi, "What in the hell took you so long?" Then Betty snatched the bag out of Gigi's hand.

Gigi gave her mom a dirty look but kept her mouth closed. Gigi opened the screen door, walked inside, and slammed the door behind her.

Betty jumped up, screaming, "You are really asking for it, little girl."

Gigi kept walking to her room.

Chapter 5

At 2 a.m. the following morning, Gigi was awakened by her dog growling. She turned towards Butch to see what was wrong. "Why are you growling?" She saw Bob standing in the doorway.

Bob started walking towards Gigi's bed, and Butch started barking. Bob said to Gigi, "I just want to talk to you for a minute if it's okay. Do you mind if I sit on the edge of your bed?"

Gigi didn't say a word, but Bob sat on the bed anyway.

Gigi said to Bob, "What do you want?" in a mean way with a dirty look on her face. Butch was still barking. Gigi told Butch to stop barking.

"I think it's time for me and you to have a little talk."

"A talk about what?"

"Me and your mom are thinking about getting married, so I'm going to be around here for a long time; I'm going to be your new daddy."

"You ain't my daddy. My daddy is on vacation. He will be back someday, and he's going to make you leave."

"I don't know why your mom told you that your daddy was on vacation. Your daddy was killed a month before you were born; he got hit by a train, walking on the railroad tracks drunk. I knew your daddy back in the day; we used to run moonshine together. That's how I met your mom. If you go to the cemetery, look for Michael T. Wilson. You will see your daddy's grave." Bob smiled. "I want you and me to become best of friends." Bob tried to rub on Gigi's leg, but she moved her leg and covered it with her nightgown.

"You're lying. Get out of my room. My daddy ain't dead. He's on vacation."

As Bob was walking out of Gigi's room, he turned towards her, lit a cigarette, and said, "You and me are going to become the best of friends, one way or another." Then he blew the cigarette smoke in the air before leaving her room.

Four hours later, at 6: a.m., Gigi was out back feeding the pigs and chickens. Betty was leaving out the front door with Bob, going to work at the coffee shop. She walked around to the side of the house and yelled out, "Gigi, when you get out of school, come by the coffee shop, do you hear me?"

"Yeah, I hear you."

After Betty and Bob took off for work, Gigi went into the house to clean herself up. She washed off all the mud that was on her feet, cleaned her face and hands, and changed her overalls. She threw her baseball cap on her head, then walked out the front door, telling Butch to stay home.

After making it to Antoinette's house, Antoinette asked her, "Where are the shoes and the clothes that you got from Miss Johnson?"

"The shoes hurt my feet; I only wear them when I have to. And I told you before, I ain't putting on no dress."

After they got out of school, Antoinette went home, and Gigi headed to the coffee shop. On the way to the coffee shop, Gigi stopped by the cemetery.

Old man Shepherd, who cut the grass and dug the holes for the cemetery, saw Gigi walking into the graveyard. He yelled out, "What do you want here?"

Gigi walked over to him. "Is a man named Michael T. Wilson buried here?"

Old man Shepherd was chewing on a mouthful of tobacco; it looked like a baseball was stuck inside of his jaw.

He spat right in front of Gigi's feet. "Your mama told me she would never tell you." Then he pointed his finger. "Yeah, he's buried right up yonder by that tree."

Gigi's eyes began to water. She took off running out of the cemetery.

Old man Shepherd yelled out, "Gigi," trying to stop her.

Gigi just kept running down the dirt road. She ran to the lake, picking up rocks and throwing them into the lake in anger.

After a few hours went by, Gigi walked to the coffee shop. She didn't care about her mom yelling at her for being late. She didn't care about anything anymore. Gigi ran into the coffee shop; the busboy Tommy was cleaning off some tables. He had a bucket full of dirty dishes sitting on the table. Gigi walked over to the table, picked up the bucket full of dirty dishes, and threw them on the floor. Pieces of broken dishes were flying everywhere, and everybody turned around to look.

Gigi yelled out to her mom, "I hate you! You told me my daddy would be coming home soon. How can he come home if he's dead?" Gigi turned and ran out of the front door.

Mr. Willard, the owner of the coffee shop, walked over to Betty. "I thought you weren't ever going to tell that child the truth about her father."

"I didn't, but I'm going to find out who did." Betty started taking off her apron and said to Mr. Willard, "I have to go find her."

Mr. Willard grabbed Betty's arm. "Let the child be for a couple of hours."

"I have to go to the bathroom for a minute." She had a bottle of whiskey behind the toilet. She grabbed the whiskey bottle, sat down on the toilet, took a couple of sips, and started crying. She took another sip, then screwed the top back on the bottle and put it back behind the toilet. She grabbed a towel to wipe the tears from her eyes, then straightened up her hair and went back to work.

Gigi was at the lake, one of her favorite places to go when she wanted to be alone. Sitting up in a tree, she watched the fish swim in the lake and played with the ants crawling on the tree limb. The sun was going down, but Gigi didn't care; normally, she'd be heading home about this time.

After Betty got off work, Bob was there to pick her up. Bob asked Betty, "What's wrong?"

"Just drive me home; I must get to the house."

Betty jumped out of the pickup truck and ran into the house, calling Gigi's name, but there was no answer. Betty asked Butch, "Do you know where Gigi is?" Butch just started barking.

Bob ran into the house. "What's going on?"

Betty was looking in all the hiding places in the house, the barn, the chicken coop, but Gigi was nowhere to be found.

Bob stopped Betty in her tracks and grabbed her by her shoulders. "What the hell is going on?"

After taking a deep breath and calming down somewhat, Betty said, "Somebody told Gigi that her daddy was dead."

"I did."

"What?" She smacked him right in his face, so hard that the right side of his cheek turned red. Betty started picking up anything she could find in the yard to throw at Bob. He tried to explain to Betty why he told Gigi about her father, but Betty didn't want to hear it.

Betty ran up the street to Antoinette's house. Antoinette's mom answered the door; her name was Mary.

"Hi Mary, is Gigi over here?"

"No, she's not over here."

"Can you ask Antoinette where she thinks Gigi might be?"

Antoinette heard her mom and Betty talking on the front porch, so she went outside. "Gigi is at the lake. That's where she always goes when she wants to be alone."

Betty ran back to the house, jumped in Bob's truck—he always left the keys in the ignition—and took off to the lake. Gigi saw the headlights from the pickup truck, and she also heard the loud noise it made when shifting gears. She knew it was Bob's truck, but she didn't care, and she stayed sitting up in that tree.

Betty parked the truck on the side of the road and then jumped out, yelling, "Gigi, Gigi, are you down here?"

Gigi didn't say a word.

As Betty got closer to the lake, she saw Gigi's feet swinging from the tree. Betty took a seat right underneath the tree. She acted like she didn't know where Gigi was, and then she started talking.

"Gigi, if you are listening, I want you to know I did not want you growing up knowing that your father was dead. I was trying to wait until you got a little older to tell you. I'm sorry you found out by somebody else telling you instead of me. Your father was a good man. Sometimes he would drink too much, but you couldn't tell him that. All he talked about was his baby girl coming into this world and all the nice things he was going to buy her. Also, all the places he was going to take you."

Gigi jumped down from the tree as Betty was talking. "I already know he got hit by a train walking on the railroad tracks."

"Well, it didn't happen the way Bob told you. His shoe got stuck, and he couldn't get it off fast enough before the train came. I still have those pair of shoes hidden in a box in my closet with your daddy's name written inside of them, also with his picture. I was trying to wait until you were twelve years old to give you his picture and tell you the truth about your father."

Gigi sat beside her mom, leaning her head on her mom's shoulder. "I'm sorry for saying all those bad things about you."

"I'm sorry for not telling you about your father sooner. Let's go home."

They jumped in the pickup truck and headed home.

Chapter 6

A few years had come and gone. Gigi was still fighting off Bob from coming into her room at peak hours in the morning. Some nights she would hide in the barn with her dog Butch. Gigi never told anybody what Bob was trying to do to her. She figured nobody would believe her, especially her mom.

Gigi would go to the graveyard some days after school and put fresh flowers on her father's grave, saying, "I wish you were here right now. Tomorrow is the Fourth of July; Antoinette and I are going to sit on top of the barn at my house and watch the fireworks shoot off into the sky. Well, I have to be going now. I have to get back home and finish my chores. I don't want Mama yelling at me. I know it's the alcohol talking when she yells at me. Sometimes I pour half of the alcohol out of the bottle then mix it with some water. I noticed she don't yell as much then. See you later, Daddy." Gigi hugged the tombstone then headed home.

After getting home and finishing her chores, she went into the house to eat dinner.

Her mom said, "After you finish eating your vittles, you boil some water and take a bath. You smell worse than the dog."

Gigi didn't say a word; she just sat there, stuffing her mouth with food and sharing her dinner with her dog Butch. After she finished eating, she did what her mom told her to do. She made sure that her dog was right by the tub in case somebody uninvited decided to walk in. After cleaning herself up, she gave Butch a bath, too. Before going to bed, she put mouse traps by her bedroom door.

About three a.m. that morning, Bob was screaming and hopping around on one foot. Gigi jumped out of bed; Butch started barking, and Betty came running into Gigi's room.

Betty said, "What the hell is going on?"

Bob fell to the floor, screaming to Betty, "Take this damn mouse trap off my toe."

Gigi was hiding on the other side of the bed, holding her mouth, and laughing.

After getting the mouse trap off Bob's toe, Betty said, "Gigi, why do you have all these damn mouse traps in this room?"

Gigi said, "To keep them out of my room."

Betty said to Bob, "What were you doing in Gigi's room at this time of the morning?"

Bob said, "I was just looking in on her, that's all."

Betty said, "Get your ass up and let me wrap that toe so it doesn't get infected."

Bob gave Gigi a dirty look and said, "I'm going to get you."

Gigi gave Bob the middle finger then stuck her tongue out.

Bob hopped into the kitchen so Betty could treat his toe.

The next morning was the Fourth of July 1938, and the town was getting ready for the big celebration. Gigi was trying to hurry up and finish her chores.

Miles across the tracks, not only was it the Fourth of July, it was also Bo's birthday. Bo's birthday was really on the third of July, but he always celebrated it on the fourth. Bo was out on the town shopping for a new suit. After finding a suit, Bo walked across the street to get his shoes shined by Mr. Glass.

They called him Mr. Glass because your shoes would look just like glass after he finished shining them.

While Bo was getting his shoes shined, everybody that passed by the shoe shop was saying, "Happy birthday, Bo," and asking when his next fight would be.

Bo was socializing with the crowd when Sophia walked up and said, "Happy birthday, Bo," and gave him a big kiss.

Everybody around them started laughing, joking, and teasing Bo, saying, "I know what your birthday present is going to be. Somebody call the fire department; this man is on fire."

While Bo and his friends were joking around, they had no idea that the sheriff and two of his deputies had just come out of the diner, having finished their lunch. The sheriff heard all the commotion across the way, and he said to his deputies, "Isn't that Sophia over there with all those colored folks?"

One of his deputies replied, "Yeah, it is."

The sheriff and his two deputies walked across the street. A few people who were standing around Bo saw the sheriff and his deputies approaching, so they quickly dispersed. As the sheriff got closer to Bo and Sophia, people started disappearing. Sophia, however, didn't care about the sheriff and stood right next to Bo as he was sitting in the shoeshine chair.

"How are you doing Bo?"

"Okay, Sheriff."

"You wouldn't happen to have a light, would you?"

Bo pulled a match out of his jacket pocket and lit it with his finger. "Here you go, Sheriff."

The sheriff, now with his pipe lit, turned his attention to Sophia. "Miss Sophia, is this colored man bothering you?"

Sophia gave the sheriff a dirty look and replied in a nasty tone, "No, this colored man is not bothering me."

"So why arc you over here with this colored man?"

"I just came to wish Bo a happy birthday just like everybody else."

"That's right, it is your birthday today. It would be a shame to spend it in jail."

Bo stared into the sheriff's eyes.

The sheriff added, "Sophia, now that you've said happy birthday, why are you still here?"

Sophia walked away up the road, and the sheriff turned back to Bo. "I got my eye on you, boy. I don't care if you are the greatest fighter in the whole damn world, you're still nothing but a colored boy in this town."

The sheriff and his deputies walked away, and Bo jumped out of the shoeshine chair. He flipped Mr. Glass a half-dollar, and Mr. Glass warned, "That white girl ain't worth it, Bo. Don't throw your life away."

Bo grabbed his suit jacket and retorted, "Mind your business, old-timer."

Five miles across the tracks, Gigi, Antoinette, and a few other kids were playing by the lake. Gigi had caught a big frog, and she ran over to Antoinette, placing the frog in her face.

Antoinette started screaming, "Get that thing away from me!" and promptly took off running.

Gigi chased Antoinette all over the place, frog still in hand, while the other kids burst into laughter. The frog eventually hopped out of Gigi's hand and landed on Antoinette's back.

She continued to scream and run, yelling, "Get it off, get it off, get it off of me!"

Gigi tried to catch up with her, but Antoinette was too fast, and she managed to get the frog off her back. However, her pretty blue dress was now covered in mud.

Exasperated, Antoinette said, "Look at my dress!"

Gigi, seemingly unfazed, asked, "What's wrong with it?"

Antoinette, angered by the state of her dress, headed home to change.

Gigi called out, "Wait up," but Antoinette paid her no mind and kept walking.

Twenty minutes later, Antoinette came back outside, and Gigi couldn't believe her eyes. Antoinette was now wearing a pair of overalls. Gigi playfully put her hand on Antoinette's forehead and asked, "Are you sick? Do you have a fever?"

Antoinette swatted Gigi's hand away. "No, I'm not sick, and I don't have a fever. I like to play with dolls; you like to play with frogs. That's why I put my overalls on."

Gigi and Antoinette returned to the lake and played until the sun went down. After sunset, they climbed on top of the barn to watch the fireworks. Gigi's mom, Betty, and her boyfriend, Bob, had gone into town to celebrate the Fourth of July.

Five miles across the tracks, Bo and Sophia were at the club, partying up a storm to celebrate the Fourth of July and Bo's birthday.

Meanwhile, the sheriff was taking a ride through the colored neighborhood and eventually made his way down to the club where the festivities were in full swing. The road was blocked with cars, so he pulled over to the side of the road and stepped out of his car, enjoying his pipe. He instructed his two deputies to check things out in the club and find out if the mayor's niece, Sophia, was in there with Bo.

The two deputies discreetly crept around the club, peering through the windows, and one of them spotted Sophia dancing with Bo. They made their way back up the road to inform the sheriff about what they had seen. The deputies hopped into their patrol car, and the sheriff remarked, "Well, boys, looks like we're going to have some fun tonight." With that, they drove off.

By 4:00 a.m., the party was winding down. Most of the partygoers had already left the club, and Bo, Sophia, and their friends were sitting at a table, sharing jokes, drinks, and cigarettes. Suddenly, a young boy named David burst into the club. Big Country, who was working at the front door, caught him by his shirt collar, lifting him off the ground.

The boy pleaded, "Put me down, Big Country, I need to see Bo."

Bo intervened, saying, "Let the boy in!"

Big Country complied, and the boy rushed over to Bo, trying to catch his breath. He had something important to tell Bo. Bo told him to catch his breath before sharing the news.

David gasped for air and requested a drink since his mouth was dry from running over. He reached for a whiskey bottle, but Bo swiftly took it from his hand. Bo asked a waitress to bring the boy a soda. After the boy had his drink, he began to speak.

"Bo, don't go home," he warned. "They're waiting for you."

"Who's waiting for me?"

"The sheriff and his deputies."

Sophia, becoming agitated, declared her intent to confront the sheriff herself. However, Bo urged her to sit down, emphasizing that was precisely what the sheriff and his deputies were hoping for. He assured her that he would handle the situation.

Everyone tried to persuade Bo not to go home, fearing the potential confrontation. Bo, however, asserted, "I don't run and hide from any man." He instructed Sophia to return home and, despite offers from Big Country and a few others to accompany him, he insisted he could handle the situation alone. Bo wanted to spare his friends from any trouble. Sophia hugged and kissed Bo, expressing her love for him, but he remained silent, choosing to head home alone.

As Bo approached the front gate of his house, he noticed the sheriff's car parked on the side of the road. The sheriff himself was sitting on the front porch, leisurely smoking his pipe, although the two deputies were not immediately visible. Bo reached his front porch, greeted the sheriff, and thanked him for the birthday wishes. He then asked why the sheriff was at his house at that early hour.

Bo's alert ears picked up the distinct sound of a shotgun being loaded. As he turned to look, two deputies emerged from behind a tree in his yard.

The sheriff inquired, "How long have you been running moonshine, Bo?"

Puzzled, Bo replied, "Moonshine? What are you talking about, Sheriff? I don't run moonshine." However, the sheriff directed his attention to a perplexing sight near the front door. There, ten cases of whiskey were stacked in wooden crates, and the sheriff questioned, "Where did all these cases of whiskey come from?"

Bo stepped back onto the porch; his frustration apparent. "Sheriff, you know that ain't my damn whiskey. What are you trying to do to me? I ain't never broken any laws in this town."

The sheriff remained unmoved. "Well, boy, I'm going to make damn sure you don't break any laws in my town. Where you're going, you won't have to worry about any laws. The only thing you're going to have to worry about is staying alive." He ordered his two deputies to handcuff Bo.

Refusing to cooperate, Bo asserted, "I ain't going nowhere. You know that damn whiskey ain't mine."

The sheriff escalated the situation by pulling out his handgun, its trigger cocked back, and threatened, "Now, boy, I'll blow your damn head right off. Don't test me. Put your damn hands behind your back."

Bo, resolute, stated, "I'd rather be dead than in prison for something I didn't do."

A scuffle ensued as the deputies attempted to handcuff Bo, but he fought back fiercely. Knocking out both deputies, Bo turned his attention to the sheriff, his determination unwavering. Out of breath, he declared, "I ain't going to jail." Bo attempted to leave through the front gate when the sheriff fired a single round from his handgun, injuring Bo's left leg. Bo cried out in pain as he fell to the ground, holding his leg. The sheriff approached him, pointing the gun between Bo's eyes, and cocked the trigger. He threatened, "I'd blow your head right off, boy, but you ain't no good to me dead." The sheriff struck Bo in the back of the neck with the handle of his gun, rendering him unconscious.

Bo regained consciousness as a bucket of cold water was thrown in his face. As he tried to assess the situation, he discovered that he was handcuffed and his feet were bound. Additionally, his left pants leg had been ripped, and his leg was bandaged.

As Bo scanned his surroundings, he realized he was confined to the holding tank in the sheriff's office. The sheriff, standing nearby, addressed him sternly. "Assault on my deputies just got you more time, boy." After delivering this message, the sheriff turned and exited the holding tank, leaving Bo alone with the deputies.

One of the deputies muttered bitterly, "You broke my damn jaw," before launching a brutal assault on Bo. The deputy rained punches down on him, and Bo crumpled to the floor, unable to defend himself due to the restraints of the handcuffs. The other deputy, not to be outdone, joined in, viciously kicking Bo while he was down. The relentless attack left Bo bloodied and battered, writhing in pain, as the deputies eventually departed, leaving him alone and injured on the floor.

Sophia pulled up at Bo's house, immediately noticing the front door wide open. Concerned, she hurriedly exited the car and rushed into the house, calling out, "Bo, where are you? Where are you?" She searched every nook and cranny of the house, but Bo was nowhere to be found.

One of the neighbors, who had ventured into Bo's yard, yelled out upon seeing Sophia, "Who is that in Bo's house?" Sophia reached the front door, and the neighbor recognized her. He commented, "Oh, it's you."

In response, Sophia inquired, "What's going on, Lil John? Have you seen Bo?"

Lil John relayed the troubling news, saying, "The sheriff took him after they shot him." He continued, "Don't act like you didn't see this day coming. You know how these white folks are. A colored man ain't got no business courting with no white girl."

Sophia hastily hopped into her car, and as she sped away, a cloud of dirt billowed behind her. Her destination: the sheriff's office, where she had one thing on her mind. Upon arriving, her car careened into the side wall of the sheriff's building, resulting in smoke emanating from under the hood and an incessantly blaring horn. The force of the collision had caused Sophia to strike her forehead on the steering wheel, and blood trickled down her face. Disoriented and injured, she managed to exit the vehicle, her movements unsteady.

The loud crash and ensuing commotion attracted the attention of passersby, who started rushing towards the scene. The sheriff and his two deputies swiftly emerged from the building, each armed with a gun. Amidst the chaos, Sophia pointed an accusatory finger at the sheriff and cried out, "You dirty bastard, why did you kill Bo?"

The onlookers grew increasingly vocal, pressing the sheriff with questions like, "Did you kill Bo?" A growing crowd, consisting of both colored and white individuals, began to assemble at the sheriff's office. The rumor that the sheriff had taken Bo's life had already begun to circulate.

Sophia reached into her purse and produced a handgun, but a nearby man of color noticed and swiftly grabbed it from her, preventing any further attention. He spoke to Sophia in an attempt to calm her down, reminding her that resorting to violence wouldn't bring Bo back but would only land her in trouble. Realizing the gravity of her actions, Sophia pushed her way through the crowd and fled, determined to escape the mounting chaos.

After breaking free from the throng, she spotted her uncle, Mr. George Thompson, the town's mayor, making his way toward the sheriff's office. The mayor was en route to address the situation when the sheriff discharged a round from his 12-gauge shotgun, commanding everyone to quiet down. Sophia reached her uncle, tears in her eyes, and, through sobs, revealed that the sheriff had killed Bo. The mayor gently removed Sophia's hands from his jacket, clearly shocked by the revelation, and expressed that this wasn't supposed to happen. In a daze, Sophia watched her uncle proceed to the sheriff's office.

As the mayor navigated through the crowd, the sheriff announced to the assembled that Bo was not deceased but locked up in his cell. A cacophony of questions erupted, demanding to know why Bo was detained. The sheriff attributed it to alleged assaults on his deputies and running moonshine. The mayor reached the office's front porch and urged everyone to disperse, assuring them he would get to the bottom of the situation. The crowd, however, was resolute, insisting they wouldn't leave until they could verify Bo was alive.

Inside the office, the mayor confronted the sheriff and his two deputies, seeking answers. The sheriff explained that they followed the mayor's instructions. The mayor inquired about Bo's whereabouts, and the sheriff revealed he was held in the holding tank. The mayor proceeded to the holding tank, where Bo stood, battered and bruised, his face bloodied, his right eye swollen shut, and blood trickling from his nose.

Bo locked eyes with the mayor and muttered, "You come on and finish what you started. I'd rather be dead than to spend the rest of my life in prison for something I didn't do." Bo's strength waned, and he collapsed to the floor, unconscious.

The mayor turned to the sheriff, scolding him, "Damn you! It's almost election time, and you take the greatest thing that's ever happened to this town and beat him to a pulp. If I don't get re-elected, you better look for a new job in a new town, Mr. Sheriff." The mayor then instructed the sheriff to send someone to fetch the doctor from across the way to clean Bo up.

Amidst this exchange, Sophia burst into the scene. She kicked one of the deputies in the leg and sprinted down the hall. Spotting her uncle and the sheriff in the corridor, they prepared to capture her, with the sheriff shouting, "Grab her, grab her! Don't let her get back there." One deputy caught her, while the other, the one she'd kicked, limped down the hall to assist in restraining her. Sophia fiercely resisted their hold, loudly demanding, "Get your damn hands off me!"

The mayor intervened, commanding them to release her, and the deputies complied, under the sheriff's gaze. Sophia then made her way toward her uncle and the sheriff and spotted Bo on the ground, blood surrounding him. She screamed at the top of her lungs, dropping to her knees while crying out Bo's name. She implored him to wake up and began rubbing his back, her concern palpable.

Bo, though injured and battered, managed to mumble, "Is that you, Sophia?"

She replied in relief, "Yes, yes, oh thank God you're not dead."

At that moment, the doctor arrived. Observing Bo's severe condition, he cast a reproachful look at the sheriff and questioned, "I made a lot of money off of this boy for all the fights he won, why in the hell did you beat him like this?"

The sheriff, unapologetic, instructed the doctor to proceed with his duties.

The sheriff and his deputies walked back down the hall. Sophia's uncle attempted to coax her to leave so the doctor could attend to Bo. Sophia exited the sheriff's office, her forehead covered in blood, and she picked up a rock from the ground, throwing it right into the sheriff's office window. The townspeople, both Black and White, began to join in, hurling objects towards the sheriff's office.

The mayor tried to calm the agitated crowd and informed them that Bo was not dead. People anxiously approached Sophia, inquiring if Bo was dead.

She replied, "No, he's not dead, but he might as well be."

The sheriff and his deputies emerged, threatening to arrest the entire town if they didn't disperse.

Sophia's uncle offered her a ride home, but she vehemently declined, asserting, "I'm not getting in no car with you. You and that damn sheriff planned this whole thing, didn't you? Didn't you?"

Her uncle retorted, "You look here, Miss Black Boy Lover. I am the damn mayor of this town, and ain't no niece of mine going to be running around this town with some colored boy."

Sophia smiled defiantly at her uncle, then confronted him directly, staring into his eyes as she stated, "Well, it looks like there's going to be a colored boy in this family, 'cause I'm having his baby."

Sophia spat right in her uncle's face and then walked away. Her uncle yelled, "Sophia, you better not have that damn baby! The family is going to disown you. Do you hear me, Sophia?"

Sophia continued walking, and that was the last time anyone in town saw her.

The townspeople were in chaos; it was akin to a riot, and the sheriff had to request assistance from across the tracks. It took more than three hours to restore order to the town. The sheriff had Bo relocated before he began filling the jail cells. He didn't bother segregating the colored from the white inmates, as far as he could see, they were all on the same side. The town was in disarray, with broken windows, litter strewn across the streets, and a few fires. More than a dozen people were injured, but fortunately, there were no fatalities.

Chapter 7

Two months had come and gone, and the whole town gathered at the courthouse, eagerly awaiting the arrival of Bo. The sheriff had kept Bo hidden until he had recovered from the terrible beating inflicted by the two deputies.

A little boy came running to the courthouse, shouting, "The sheriff is coming, the sheriff is coming, and he's got Bo chained up in the back of his truck!"

Nobody had seen Bo since his birthday, and the town was filled with anxiety. When the townspeople saw the sheriff's truck approaching on the dirt road, they started running towards it, calling out, "Bo, Bo, you're alive, you're alive!"

Bo's parents and two sisters stood by the courthouse; their eyes filled with tears as they spotted him.

Bo was in the back of the truck with the two deputies, who had 12-gauge shotguns pointed at the crowd. They escorted Bo off the truck, demanding that everyone make way. Bo's hands and ankles were chained.

As he made his way through the crowd, a couple of white boys spat on him and yelled, "Hang that boy!"

The crowd started growing unruly, and the sheriff urged his deputies to hurry and get Bo inside before another riot could break out. Bo scanned the crowd, but the one face he longed to see was conspicuously absent.

The courtroom only permitted Bo's parents and his two sisters among the colored people. After hearing all the charges brought against Bo on September 3, 1938, the judge sentenced him to twenty years of hard labor.

Bo leaped up, exclaiming, "Those are all lies! You know I didn't do any of those things!"

The judge ordered Bo to be silenced and removed from the courtroom, and so he was sent to prison, assigned to the Chain Gang.

After Bo's departure, the town fell into a cold silence, and things began to revert to the way they used to be. Colored people stayed on their side of the road, and white folks stayed on theirs.

You would hear people sitting around talking about Bo, how good of a fighter he was, especially the time he fought Big Country. As time moved on, the mayor was not re-elected. There were a lot of White folks who liked Bo. The new mayor, Mr. Dean Harrison, fired the sheriff and his two deputies. He appointed a new sheriff and two new deputies who were not racist.

CHAPTER 8

Two and a half years had come and gone. The year was 1945. Five miles across the tracks, Gigi was nine and a half years old, soon to be ten. It was the first day of spring. Gigi and Antoinette were on their way home from school, and as Gigi got closer to her house, they heard a gunshot.

Antoinette said, "That sounded like it came from your house."

"It did, didn't it?"

They both took off running towards the house. They ran through the front yard into the house and didn't see anybody. They ran in the backyard, and Gigi saw her mom and Bob standing by the chicken coop.

Gigi ran over and said, "What's going on?" She looked down on the ground and saw her dog, Butch; he was dead, and Bob had a shotgun in his hands. Gigi picked up a piece of wood that was laying on the ground and swung it at Bob's legs, striking him right in his knees. Bob fell to the ground screaming, and Gigi just kept striking Bob with the piece of wood, yelling, "You killed my dog! You killed my dog."

Betty and Antoinette were trying to stop Gigi from hitting Bob. Before they could stop her, Bob backslapped Gigi right in her face. She hit the ground, and Betty yelled, "Stop it! Stop it!"

Gigi jumped up, wiped the blood from her mouth, and took off running. Antoinette took off right behind her. Betty was yelling, "Gigi, you come back here this minute!"

After running about a half mile down the road, Gigi stopped running.

Antoinette said, "Thank you, I needed to catch my breath."

"I'm not going back there."

"Well, what are you going to do?"

"I don't know. I pray to God every night, but I guess I'm not praying loud enough."

Antoinette took Gigi to her house, and she asked her mom if Gigi could spend the night.

Antoinette's mom said, "You both have school tomorrow; she can stay for supper, after that, you have to go home."

Gigi said, "Yes, ma'am."

After supper, Antoinette asked Gigi what she was going to do.

"Don't worry about me; I'll see you later."

"Will you be coming to school tomorrow?"

"Yes, I'll see you in school." Gigi took off walking down the dark dirt road. When she got home, she saw her mom and Bob sitting on the front porch, drinking and smoking cigarettes. So, she snuck around the back of the house, walked over by the chicken coop, and noticed Butch was gone. She found an old truck tire and rolled it underneath her bedroom window so she could climb in.

After she got in her room, she just sat on the edge of the bed, twiddling her fingers. Then she lay on the bed, looked up at the ceiling, and said, "God, can you hear me? I've been talking to you since I was five years old. How come you never answer me? Are you still here with me?" Then a big wind came through Gigi's bedroom window, slamming her bedroom door.

It was so loud that her mom heard the door slam, and she yelled, "Gigi, you go in there and eat your dinner, wash up, and go to bed. You have school tomorrow. You hear me, Gigi?"

"Yes, ma'am." Gigi took her food out back and gave it to the pigs; she had already eaten. Gigi washed up and went to bed.

Her mom walked into the room and said, "We had to put Butch down because he got into a fight with the wolf that was trying to steal the chickens. The wolf bit Butch up bad. We buried him on the other side of the barn where he used to go and lay when it was too hot outside."

Gigi didn't say a word, and her mom walked out of the room, smoking her cigarette. Gigi didn't go to sleep for a few hours; the room felt empty without her dog, Butch, in there.

Two months later, on June 4, it was Gigi's birthday. Gigi was out back feeding the chickens when her mom yelled out the window. "Gigi, get in here and wash up so we can head into town." After Gigi washed up, her mom said, "Put this on and these socks and shoes. You're ten years old now. Time to start looking like a young lady." Gigi mumbled something, and her mom said, "What was that? Did you say something?"

"No, ma'am."

After getting dressed and her hair combed, Gigi was unrecognizable.

Her mom said, "Oh, look at my little angel." She yelled, "Bob, come look at Gigi! Doesn't she look like a little princess?"

"Yeah, she looks real good."

Gigi gave Bob a dirty look, and he was just standing there smiling.

Betty said, "Okay, let's go, get in the truck."

When they got to town, Betty asked Gigi, "Do you want me to make you a cake or buy one?"

Gigi said, "The last cake you made me had a big dent in the middle of it."

"Okay, I think I will buy you a cake this year."

Everywhere they went, everyone was asking Betty who the little girl was and where was Gigi. They couldn't believe the little girl they saw was Gigi, who was giving everybody a dirty look and complaining that her shoes were hurting her feet.

Betty said, "Better those shoes than your bottom."

They were having Gigi's birthday party at the coffee shop. Mr. Willard, the owner of the shop, who always looked at Gigi as his good luck charm, asked Betty, "Who is the little girl and where is Gigi?"

Gigi stomped on Mr. Willard's foot with her right shoe, and he screamed. Gigi said, "I'm right here," then she crossed her arms and stuck out her lip.

Mr. Willard said, "Oh my God, is that you?"

Gigi said, "Well, it's not a ghost."

Betty burst out laughing and told Gigi to help her put the candles on the cake. While Gigi was putting the candles on the cake, Antoinette walked in and screamed, "Oh my God, Gigi, look at you!"

"It's good to know that somebody recognizes me."

Gigi had on a pink dress, white socks, and black shoes, and her hair was combed, and her face wasn't dirty. After the rest of the kids showed up, they sang happy birthday to Gigi, and she opened her presents. She had more baby dolls than anything else, but Gigi didn't play with dolls, so with a frown on her face, she left them laying on the table.

Bob came from the kitchen and yelled, "Look what I found back here!" It was a female German Shepherd puppy with a pink bow around her neck.

Gigi's eyes lit up like a Christmas tree, and that frown turned into a smile as she went running over to grab the puppy. While she was holding the puppy up in the air, it peed on her dress. Gigi didn't care, but Betty was mad, and she yelled, "I just bought that damn dress!"

Everybody started laughing, and Gigi was happy to take that dress off and put her overalls on; she was back to her old self.

Antoinette said, "What are you going to name her?"

"Abby, that's what I'm going to call her, Abby."

Antoinette said, "That's a nice name, I like that."

After the party, everybody went their separate ways. Gigi jumped in the back of the pickup truck with the puppy in her arms while Bob drove them home.

Chapter 9

Six a.m. sunrise, five miles across the tracks, the guards at the Mississippi State Prison were waking up all of the prisoners that were on the Chain Gang. Bo was one of them. As they all lined up outside, the guards chained two prisoners together at a time. There were over seventy-five prisoners for outside work, and Bo was chained to a man they called Kobe. Kobe was serving thirty years for armed robbery and the kidnapping of a White girl. Bo and Kobe had to work as a team since they were chained together.

Today's assignment for the prisoners was to clear a field of high grass that was five miles long. It took over an hour before the prisoners reached the field where they had to work. The sun was already beating down on them. The prison guards escorted all of the convicts off the truck and gave them tools to work with.

The captain of the guards yelled out to the prisoners, "I don't want to be out here all damn day, so all of you cookies get to work."

While Bo and Kobe were working, Kobe said, "I found a way we can get out of here."

"Well, you won't get far before they shoot you in the back."

"I'm talking about after midnight."

"The chains are not long enough to run, how are you going to get away?"

"I'll show you when we get back."

It took from sunup to sundown to clear that high field of grass. While waiting in line for a drink of water, the train was going by.

Kobe said, "That's our ticket right there."

Bo was staring at the train as it went by.

One of the guards pushed Bo in the back and said, "Get your ass on the truck, convict."

Bo didn't want to spend the night in the hotbox, so he did what the guard told him to do.

After getting back to the prison camp and cooling off from the hot sun, it was chow time. Kobe was going over the escape plan with Bo. He told him that the wood under his bed was already fixed for them to escape. The guards walked around the campus every thirty minutes, and there's a train that comes by at four a.m. on the dot every morning. "It's going to take us about forty minutes to an hour to run five miles, so we have to already be in the woods by three o'clock."

"How are we going to get over that fence?"

"Who said we're going over the fence?"

"What about these chains?"

"Come bedtime, I got something for you. We have all night to work on it."

Friday evening, and 9:00 p.m., the prison guard walked in. "All right, convicts, lights out."

Kobe whispered to Bo, "It's time." He pulled out a metal file.

"How did you get your hands on that?"

"When you've been here as long as I have, you can get your hands on almost anything." Kobe started filing the chain between his legs. It took him over thirty minutes, and then he tied the chain around his legs with a piece of torn cloth. It was Bo's turn; it took him about the same length of time to break the chain between his legs. He then tied the chain around his leg with a piece of cloth.

Five miles across the tracks, it was ten o'clock at night. Gigi was in her bed sleeping with her puppy by her side. Betty had to work late at the coffee shop because one the waitresses called in sick. Bob was on the front porch drinking more than usual.

Gigi and the dog were awakened by a bottle breaking. Bob had dropped it on the front porch. Gigi jumped out of bed and ran to the front porch; her dog ran right behind her. Bob was laid out on the porch. Gigi hit Bob in his back telling him to get up and go to bed. Bob didn't move.

Gigi went into the kitchen and came back with a bucket of cold water. She poured the water right on Bob's head. "Wake up, you old drunken fool."

Bob jumped up, wiping the water off his face. As he looked around, he saw three Gigi's because he was so drunk. "Gigi, I didn't know you had two sisters, they look just like you."

"Get up and go to bed, I'm going to tell mama that you drank a whole bottle of whiskey."

As Gigi turned around to walk back into the house, Bob grabbed her ankle.

"Get off of me!"

Bob pulled Gigi to the wooden floorboards of the porch. She was trying to kick herself free, but Bob wouldn't let her go.

Bob took his other hand and pulled her nightgown and started ripping it off.

Gigi screamed, "Get off me! Get off me! What are you doing?"

"It's time I teach you some manners." He smacked Gigi right in the face, her head hitting the porch. She played like she was out cold. Bob stood up over Gigi, took off his shirt and threw it in the yard. He started unbuckling his belt. As he kneeled down over Gigi, he said, "Your mama can't save your ass now, you're mine."

Gigi opened her eyes and took her foot and kicked Bob right in the crotch. Bob's eyes got wider than an owl's. He was in so much pain he couldn't even scream. Then Gigi kicked him right in the chest, and Bob went flying backwards, holding his crotch. Gigi jumped up and ran into her bedroom.

Bob screamed, "I'm going to get you, you little bitch!"

Gigi grabbed her overalls and her hat, picked up the puppy, and climbed out the bedroom window. The only place she knew she could go was to Antoinette's.

As she was running up the dirt road, she could hear Bob shooting off his gun, screaming, "I'm going to kill you!"

Gigi didn't look back; she just kept running. After making it to Antoinette's house, she snuck around the back where Antoinette's bedroom was. The dogs started barking, and

Antoinette heard them. She jumped out of bed to look out the back window and saw Gigi.

Antoinette said, "What are you doing here, Gigi? What's going on?" After helping Gigi climb through the bedroom window, Gigi told her what Bob had tried to do to her.

"I'm not going back there," Gigi said.

"You have to tell your mom."

"No, she won't believe me."

Gigi and Antoinette talked most of the night, trying to figure out what to do next.

Gigi said, "I think I'm going to go to Alabama and stay with my grandma."

"How are you going to get there?"

"I haven't thought of that yet."

Five miles across the tracks, it was 2:40 a.m. As Bo and Kobe were crawling through the hole in the floor, all the other prisoners wished them luck. They were too afraid to go.

As they made their way to the back fence, they had to keep a lookout for the prison guards and the spotlight that comes around every fifteen minutes. After digging the hole under the fence, Bo went under first, then Kobe.

Kobe said, "You smell that?"

"Smell what?"

"Freedom."

They took off running through the woods.

At 3:30 a.m., Bo and Kobe stopped running to catch their breath.

Bo said, "You hear that?"

"Hear what?"

"Sounds like dogs."

Kobe said, "Oh shit, they're onto us. We have to make it across the creek, then we'll be almost to the tracks."

As Bo and Kobe ran through the woods, trying to outrun the dogs, Kobe stepped into a big hole, breaking his leg in half. You could see his leg bone sticking straight up through the skin. Kobe screamed so loud you could hear him a mile away.

Bo was trying to help Kobe. Kobe said, "I'm done, look at my leg, go ahead, Bo, you're not supposed to be here anyway. I wish you luck; now get on. Those dogs are getting closer."

"It was nice knowing you, man. I hope I don't see you again."

Kobe started laughing, then Bo started laughing.

Kobe said, "Here, man, take this." It was a cigar he was going to share with Bo when they got on that train. "When you get on that train, Bo, take a pull for me."

"For sure, old friend."

Kobe started crying. As Bo ran through the woods, he didn't look back. He could hear the horn of the train coming. As Bo ran across the creek, he heard a shotgun go off. He knew they had found Kobe.

Five miles across the tracks, Gigi heard the train horn. She jumped up and said, "That's it."

Antoinette asked, "What's it?"

"The train. I'm going to take the train to Alabama."

"Gigi, you have gone cuckoo. You don't even know which way Alabama is. You don't even know if that train goes to Alabama."

"I don't care. I'm getting on that train. I need you to watch Abby for me."

"You're really going to get on that train."

"Yes, I am."

"You don't have any food. Let me sneak in the kitchen and grab you some things."

Antoinette gave Gigi a bag of food, then a big hug. The train horn sounded again.

"I have to go. I've got to catch that train."

As Gigi was climbing out of the bedroom window, Antoinette said, "Good luck. I'm really going to miss you."

"You must promise me that you won't tell anybody. Pinky promise me."

Antoinette pinky-promised, but she had her fingers crossed.

Gigi ran through the backyard and into the woods.

Five miles down the track, Bo was hiding behind a tree until half of the cargo train passed by. He saw one of the doors open and took off running towards the train. He didn't have to run too fast because the train was only going about twenty miles an hour. After making it onto the train, Bo stood in the doorway, looking through the woods. He could see the flashlights and hear the dogs, but they were too far back to catch him, so he knew he was safe.

Five miles up the track, Gigi only had to run a mile to reach the railroad tracks. But first, she had to get across the lake. Gigi knew how to cross the lake without getting wet; an old tree had fallen across the lake many years ago. She just had to be careful not to slip and fall from all the algae covering the dead tree. At 4:15 a.m., the train's horn sounded off again. Gigi knew she had to hurry up because the train was getting closer.

After making it across the lake and traveling half a mile through the woods, she was able to see the train passing by. Gigi was saying to herself, "How am I going to get on this train?" Then she spotted a cargo door open. Gigi took off running, throwing her bag of food into the open door before hopping inside. The darkness was overwhelming, so she had to feel around on the floor to find her bag of food. After finding her food, she took her ponytail and stuffed it down the back of her shirt. Then she pulled her baseball cap way down over her head so nobody would know that she was a little girl.

Gigi stood in front of the open cargo doorway, looking at the passing scenery. Out of nowhere, she spotted two men running for the train. She said to herself, "Oh no, I have to get out of sight." She hid behind the cargo door, then peeked out and saw the two men running right to the open cargo door where she was. She tried to close the door, but it was jammed, so she hid in a corner.

Her heart was beating so fast she started sweating. The two men jumped into the cargo car. Billy and Tiny were two hillbilly boys always looking for trouble. The only thing, the one they called Tiny was anything but that. He weighed two-hundred-forty pounds and was six-foot-six. After finding a spot to sit down, Billy and Tiny started talking and drinking. They pulled out a black bottle of moonshine, then fired up some cigarettes.

The smoke from the cigarettes made Gigi sneeze.

Tiny said, "Gesundheit."

Gigi said, "Thank you." Then Gigi put her hand over her mouth, saying to herself, "Oh no."

Billy jumped up and said, "Wait a minute, who else is on this train? Show yourself." Billy struck a match; he saw Gigi sitting in the corner. "Stand up, boy. You're too young to be hitchhiking on this train. How old are you, boy?"

Gigi was trying to disguise her voice to sound like a boy. She said in a deep voice, "I'm ten."

The match was burning out. Billy said to Tiny, "Hand me a candle out of my bag." Billy struck another match, then he lit the candle. After seeing the bag Gigi was holding in her hand, Billy said, "What you got in that bag, boy?"

Gigi said, "My dirty laundry."

Billy snatched the bag out of Gigi's hand.

"Give me back my bag, you old stinky man." Gigi tried to grab her bag; Billy smacked her down to the floor.

Billy said, "Tiny, we got us some dinner." Then they heard the sound of some chains moving. "Who's that? Who else is here?" Billy pointed the candle in the direction of the noise. He saw a colored man sitting on the floor with a prison uniform on and chains tied around his legs. That man was Bo.

Bo pulled out the cigar that Kobe had given him, stuck it in his mouth, then said, "May I have a light?"

Billy started laughing. "Tiny, look at what we got here. We got us a fugitive. I know there's a reward out for you, boy, and me and my cousin Tiny are going to get that reward." Billy pulled out a pocketknife and told Tiny to hold the candle.

As Bo was standing up, he said, "I don't want no trouble."

Billy said, "Won't be no trouble if you do what I tell you to do, boy. We getting off this train at the next town. Now you just sit your Black ass back down."

Gigi yelled, "Leave him alone, he ain't bothering you!"

Billy turned his head to tell Gigi to shut up; Bo saw his opportunity. He grabbed the knife from Billy then punched him in the face. Billy went flying backward. Tiny was trying to help Billy up. Billy said, "You just committed suicide, boy." Billy wiped the blood from his mouth then said to Tiny, "Dead or alive, we still get some money."

Tiny charged at Bo saying, "You're dead, boy." As he tried to grab Bo, Bo moved out of the way and Tiny ran into the wall. As he turned around to face Bo, Bo started punching him everywhere. The final blow was to his stomach that sent Tiny falling to the floor.

As Bo was walking over to Billy, Billy jumped off the train. Bo dragged Tiny to the open door, told him, "Get up and get off before I throw you off."

Tiny said, "Okay, man, okay, I'm getting off." Tiny stood up in front of the doorway. He was taking too long to jump off, so Bo kicked him in his butt. Tiny went flying off the train, screaming out, "Billy, help me!"

Bo took a seat in front of the open cargo door to keep an eye out for any more drifters.

Gigi walked over and said, "Thank you, mister."

"You talk funny for a boy."

Gigi forgot to disguise her voice, then she said in a deep voice, "That's my allergies; it makes me talk funny sometimes." Gigi said, "Are you hungry? I have some food."

Bo said, "What are you doing on this train, boy?"

Gigi said, "I'm going to see my grandma; she stays in Alabama."

"How do you know this train goes to Alabama?"

"My best friend Antoinette told me." Gigi pulled out some sandwiches that she'd gotten from Antoinette.

While she and Bo were eating, Gigi said, "Mister, did you escape from the prison? Are you a fugitive for real?"

Bo said, "They threw me in jail for something I didn't do; I'm innocent. They were just mad because my girlfriend was a White girl."

Gigi said, "If two people like each other, no matter what color they are, they should be able to be friends."

Bo said, "I like you already, boy."

Gigi just smiled.

As the darkness turned to daylight, Gigi and Bo had fallen asleep. Bo was awakened by the train stopping. He jumped up, looked out the doorway, and saw some men with some dogs coming his way.

He said, "See you in the next life, kid," then jumped off the train and ran into the woods.

Gigi jumped up; before she could say anything, Bo was gone into the woods. Gigi grabbed her bag, peeked out the cargo door to see if the coast was clear, then jumped off the train and ran into the woods. As she was running through the woods, she was screaming, "Mister, mister, where are you?"

Bo was hiding behind a tree. When Gigi passed him, he grabbed her, then put his hand over her mouth and said, "Shut up, kid. You're trying to get me caught?" Bo started running through the woods.

"Wait for me."

"Don't follow me, kid; find your own way." Bo started running faster through the woods until he couldn't see Gigi anymore.

She tried her hardest to keep up, but Bo was running too fast. Gigi stopped to catch her breath. As she was looking down, she could see shoe prints in the ground. Gigi followed the shoe prints for over an hour. She noticed that the shoe prints were not deep in the ground like they were before, so she knew that Bo had stopped running.

After catching up with Bo, she saw him hiding behind the bushes, staring at something. She walked up behind him; Bo turned around and then whispered, "How in the hell did you find me, boy?"

Gigi disguised her voice once again. "I followed your shoe prints in the ground."

"Go over to that house and see if somebody's in there."

Gigi said, "No."

"Do as I tell you, boy, now get."

Gigi took a seat on a big rock. "I'm not going anywhere until you apologize to me."

Bo bit his lip, "Okay, boy, I apologize. Now get over there and see if someone is in that house."

Gigi said, "You didn't say please."

Bo jumped up and raised his hand.

"Okay, okay, I'm going, calm down."

Bo gave Gigi a dirty look as she walked past him. Gigi walked in the house, then yelled out the broken window, "Nobody's in here. Come on."

Before Bo walked into the house, he walked around the yard, looking for tools to finish breaking the chain that was strapped to each one of his ankles. After looking in the old shack, he found what he needed. He took the tools then walked in the house. Bo saw an old washtub and he had found some clothes. "Boy, go out there and see if you can find some water, while I get a fire started."

As Gigi was walking out the front door, Bo said, "By the way, what's your name, boy?"

"My name is Tommy. People call me Tom." She walked out the front door.

While Bo was starting a fire in the old fireplace, Gigi found a water well. She threw a big rock down there to see if there was any water. After hearing a splash, she ran back into the house. "Mister, mister, I found some water, but we will need a long rope and a bucket."

Bo searched around everywhere for rope, but didn't find any. He did find a lot of old rags and a bucket.

He tied all the rags together, then attached the bucket to one end. The rags were long enough to reach the water. After pulling up the first bucket of water, he took it inside the house and poured it into the washtub to clean out the dirt. After collecting enough water to fill the washtub, Bo heated the water up. Once it was hot enough, he poured it into the washtub.

"Boy, get in there, take them rags off, you smell as bad as I do. The dogs will find us for sure; and don't take all day, I'll be back."

Bo went into the woods to find something to eat. Gigi waited until she saw Bo walk into the woods, then she took her clothes off and jumped into the tub. She felt so good sitting in that tub of water that she forgot she had to hurry up and finish before Bo returned. She ended up falling asleep. After thirty minutes had passed, Gigi woke up, looked around, and said, "Oh no, I have to get out of this tub."

As she was getting out of the tub, Bo walked in holding a rabbit in his hand, and he saw Gigi standing there butt naked. He dropped the rabbit out of his hand. "You, you, you, you not no damn boy, you a little girl." As Bo was walking out the house, he said, "Oh God, they going to hang me for sure. They're going to lynch me; they're going to cut my head off!"

Gigi put on her clothes as fast as she could, and caught up with Bo. "Please, please, mister, please. I didn't want anybody to know I was a girl."

"It's bad enough that you are white, but also a little girl. Get away from me. I'm already in enough trouble." Bo just kept walking through the woods.

Gigi stopped walking, then said, while crying, "I ran away from home. My mama's boyfriend tried to rape me. I'm trying to get to Alabama to my grandma's house."

Bo stopped walking, turned around to face Gigi. She was leaning up against a tree, crying. Bo walked over to Gigi. He didn't know what to say. "Come on, boy, I mean, girl." They walked back to the house.

Bo had skinned and cooked the rabbit he caught in the woods.

Gigi said, "This tastes good."

"Everything tastes good when you're starving."

After eating, Bo found enough materials for Gigi to sleep on, piling them up by the fireplace. "You sleep over here."

"Where are you going to sleep?"

"Who said I was going to sleep? Now you go and get some shut-eye; we may have to leave soon."

Gigi excitedly said, "You said 'we,' so that means you're taking me with you." She jumped up and ran over to hug Bo.

"Don't count your chickens before they hatch. I'm just going to do my best to get you on that train to Alabama." Then he looked up at the sky through the hole in the roof and said, "Oh God, what have I gotten myself into."

After Gigi fell asleep, Bo took a bath and changed his clothes. He then walked into the woods and climbed up a tree. The tree was tall enough to see all around the house, and that's where Bo stayed until sunrise.

Back in town, Gigi's mom Betty found out what was going on from talking to Antoinette. Betty had beaten Bob half to death with a cast iron skillet. He took off in his pickup truck and never came back. The sheriff and half of the town were looking for Gigi. Betty had called her mother in Alabama, telling her that Gigi had run away and might be headed her way. Betty said, "Just keep her there until I get there." Betty's mom agreed.

The sheriff had found out that there was also an escaped convict on the loose, and that two hillbilly boys, Billy and Tiny, were on the train with the convict and a little White boy. Betty was asking the sheriff what the little White boy had on. The sheriff said, "Some overalls, a tee shirt, and a baseball cap."

Betty started screaming, "That ain't no little boy, that's Gigi. Oh God, we have to find my child, she's with that convict."

The sheriff was calling all counties to be on the lookout for a Black male who had escaped from the penitentiary, goes by the name of Bo, and a little White girl looking like a boy who goes by the name of Gigi. The warden and guards from the prison were stopping all cargo trains, checking them for the fugitive Bo and Gigi.

Chapter 10

Come sunrise, Gigi had awakened from sleeping all night, and as she looked around, she realized Bo was nowhere to be seen. She ran outside, calling, "Mister, mister, where are you?"

Bo's voice suddenly cut through, stern and gruff, "You scream one more time, and I'm going to cut your damn tongue out and eat it for breakfast."

Gigi, a bit shaken, responded, "I thought you left me."

"What if I did? You've got two legs, you've got two feet, you've got two eyes to see, and you have a brain. If you can't depend on yourself, you can't depend on nobody. Don't you ever forget that, and my name is Bo, not mister."

Gigi, trying to lighten the mood, added, "How does that taste?"

Bo couldn't help but burst into laughter, and soon enough, Gigi joined in.

Bo and Gigi walked for miles until they came across a small, unfamiliar hick town that wasn't even on the map.

"I ain't never heard about this place before."

Gigi agreed, saying, "Me either."

"You're going to have to go into town and find us something to eat, while I stay here in these woods. Just take what you can find and try not to get caught."

"I don't have to steal nothing." She sat down on the ground, pulled her boots off, turned them upside down, and money fell onto the ground.

"Well, cut me twice, and I'll say ouch." He then grabbed Gigi, kissed her on her forehead, and praised her. "You're a lifesaver, kid."

"I've been saving my money since I was five years old."

"Put some money in your pocket and put the rest back in your boots. Try not to talk to anybody. You have to remember, they may be looking for us, so you're going to have to act like a little boy again."

"Okay, I'll be back."

As Gigi walked through town, a little boy named Petey ran up to her, asking, "Hey, what's your name? I've never seen you around here before."

"I'm just passing through. My name is Tommy."

Petey found her speech unusual. "You talk funny, you got a frog in your throat or something?"

"No, I'm just a little hoarse."

"Well, my name is Petey; everybody calls me Pete. So where are you heading?"

"I'm looking for a store to buy some food."

"Follow me, I'll take you to Mrs. Bee's. She's got the best food in town. By the way, where are your mom and paw?"

"They're somewhere around here. They sent me to go get the food, and if you quit asking so many questions, I'll buy you a burger."

"With cheese on it?"

"Yes, with cheese on it."

Inside Mrs. Bee's place, Petey and Gigi ordered their burgers. Petey realized he'd forgotten Gigi's family and corrected the order to four burgers with cheese. Mrs. Bee took their request and began preparing the food.

While waiting for their burgers, a man in a fancy suit walked in and approached the counter where Gigi and Petey were sitting. He asked the kids how they were doing, and Petey replied, "We're doing fine." The man wanted to know who owned the place, and Petey explained, "Mrs. Bee. She's in the back making us some burgers. I'll call her for you." He shouted for Mrs. Bee, and she soon emerged from the back.

"What can I do for you, mister?"

The man pulled out a badge, showing it to Mrs. Bee. "Have you seen a little Caucasian girl around ten years old and a Black man walking together around these parts?"

"I haven't seen any strangers come in here all morning."

As Gigi listened, she pulled her cap down over her eyes and held her head down.

The man gave Mrs. Bee a contact number. "If you do see them, call this number." He handed her a piece of paper with the number and left the store.

After the man's departure, Gigi asked Mrs. Bee, "Are those burgers ready yet?"

Mrs. Bee promised, "Count to ten, and I'll be right back."

She returned with the burgers, and Petey mentioned, "Where are you going, Tommy? You don't want to eat in here?"

"No, I've got to be getting on." Petey offered to walk her back, and Gigi accepted, thanking him after they left Mrs. Bee's.

Gigi said goodbye to Petey, and after leaving the store, she sneaked back into the woods without being seen. She started calling for Bo, and leaves from a tree began falling on her head. Looking up, she saw Bo's feet. Gigi playfully teased, "I bet when you were a kid and played hide and seek, nobody ever found you."

Bo jumped down from the tree. "You're right. Whatever is in that bag is going to hide in my stomach, and no one will find it."

Gigi chuckled. "Okay." Gigi told Bo she had brought two burgers for him and one for herself.

While they were eating, Bo explained, "We're going to have to steal us a car."

"I thought we were going to catch another train."

"They will be checking out all of the trains, so that's out. We'll camp out here and wait until the town goes to sleep before we make our move."

At 2:45 a.m., the little hick town had gone to sleep, and there was nobody walking around. Bo woke Gigi up, and they started to move through the town. Bo pointed at a vehicle. "We'll take this one."

"I don't like that one. I like that one over there."

"Get in the car."

"No."

Bo sighed. "I wish you were a boy for real. You girls are hard to please. Come on."

Bo and Gigi crept over to the car Gigi liked. Bo instructed her, "Now get behind the steering wheel, keep the wheel straight." Gigi followed his command, and Bo got behind the car, pushed it away from the house, and started the engine. He said, "Move over," then started driving down the road. However, the car started making loud popping sounds, similar to gunshots, and began jerking back and forth. Bo expressed his frustration. "I knew I shouldn't have listened to you; you picked the worst damn car on the street."

"But it's a pretty color, just a little noisy."

Bo just shook his head, and they continued down the dirt road.

As the sun was coming up, Bo saw a sign that read "Alabama, 42 miles ahead." He knew the car wasn't going to make it another hour on the road.

A few miles up the road, Gigi said, "Bo, look over there." They saw a small house with a gas pump in front of it.

Bo told Gigi, "Pull a few dollars out of your boot, then jump in the back seat and cover yourself up."

"Okay."

As Bo pulled up in front of the gas pump, a teenage boy came out of the house; his name was Benny. Bo got out of the car and said, "Howdy."

"What can I do for you?"

"I'll be needing some gas."

Benny started laughing. "Well, you ain't going to get no gas from that pump; the only thing that pump is full of is dirt."

"How far is the next town?"

"About fifteen miles up the road. When you come to the fork, stay to the left."

As Bo was getting back into the car, Gigi whispered to Bo, "See if they have something to eat and something to drink."

"By any chance, would you have some food and water I can buy from you?"

Gigi whispered again, "I want a soda pop and some candy," but Bo whispered back to her, "Shut up."

Benny said, "Come on in."

As Bo walked into the house, he saw an old man sitting in a rocking chair, choking while smoking a cigarette. The old man was Benny's father, Mr. Kramer. Mr. Kramer said, "Who let that colored boy in my house? Get that colored boy out of my damn house."

Benny said, "Shut up, old man," then said to Bo, "Don't pay my father no mind; his best friend was a colored man. Give him a few minutes; he'll be asking you to sit down and smoke a cigarette with him, then talk your ear off. He goes in and out; they say he has Alzheimer's, whatever that means.

Well, this is all we have right here. Here's a case of soda pop, not cold though."

Bo grabbed what he could and paid Benny.

As he was walking out the door, Mr. Kramer said, "Hey, boy, come over here and sit down and have a cigarette with me."

Benny said, "I told you."

Bo replied, "Next time, old-timer."

Mr. Kramer said, "Keep the princess safe; she's your future."

Benny said, "Don't pay my father no mind; he's cuckoo."

Bo walked out the front door with the bag of groceries, jumped in the car, and drove off. He couldn't take his mind off what Mr. Kramer had said to him. Gigi jumped back into the front seat, digging into the bag to see what Bo had bought and running her mouth at the same time. Bo wasn't paying Gigi any mind; he was still thinking about the message he received from Mr. Kramer.

A few miles up the road, the car cut off and began coasting down the road.

Gigi said, "Oh wow, the Lord answered my prayers. I said, 'God, please take this loud noise away from this car.'"

"Yeah, and He also took the gas."

"What? Are we out of gas?"

"Grab your belongings; we've got to keep moving. If we had taken the main road, we wouldn't have too far to go." Bo continued, "We have to stay off the main roads; that's why we're on this back road, and we still have to be careful."

As Gigi and Bo were walking, they heard a vehicle coming up behind them. Bo told Gigi, "Quick, get behind me." As the truck pulled up, Bo was relieved to see that a colored man was driving it, with a truck load of chickens in crates. Bo said, "Howdy."

"How do. Is that your car back yonder?"

"No, but I'll be needing a lift though."

"If you can find room back there, you're welcome to ride."

"That's mighty kind of you, mister. What's your name?"

"Everybody calls me Smokey. What's your name, boy?"

"Everybody calls me Bo."

"Wait a minute, the only Bo I know of is doing time in prison, never seen him though. I heard he was the baddest street fighter to ever walk the streets."

"Well, I'm the other Bo that's not locked up."

"I sure wish I could have met him. You and your boy hop on in."

Smokey didn't see Gigi; all he saw was some overalls and a baseball cap. While riding in the back of the truck, the chicken feathers were flying everywhere. Gigi was pulling the feathers from her face, and every time she pulled one off, it would fly on Bo.

Bo said, "Keep your feathers to yourself," and threw them back on Gigi. Before they knew it, they started having a feather fight and both burst into laughter.

"Is it true what that man said about you? You were the greatest street fighter. No wonder you were able to beat those two men up on the train."

Bo began telling Gigi about his life, how he got started, and before they knew it, they were approaching the fork in the road. The truck started slowing down, and Bo stood up to see what was going on. There were a bunch of cars and trucks in front of them, and he saw the sheriff's car. A group of deputies was checking vehicles at the fork in the road.

Gigi asked, "What's going on? Why did we stop?"

"It's not good; we have to make it to the woods."

Bo thanked Smokey for the ride and asked him not to mention seeing them. Smokey understood the situation and knew what to say when the sheriff came to check his truck. Bo also added, "By the way, you did meet the real Bo." They jumped off the back of the truck and ran back a few yards, then tucked themselves into the high bushes. Bo told Gigi to stay behind him and stay low as they passed the checkpoint through the high bushes. Bo urged Gigi to start running.

CHAPTER 11

Back in town, Betty and some friends of hers, Mr. Willard and Mimi, were out driving everywhere looking for Gigi. Mimi knew about a town that wasn't on the map, and she showed them how to get there. After arriving in the town, Betty instructed everyone to spread out and ask people if they had seen a little White girl who looked like a boy, accompanied by a colored man. Mimi suggested that Betty accompany her to Mrs. Bee's cookhouse, where they hadn't seen each other in quite a while.

In the cookhouse, Mrs. Bee and Mimi shared a warm greeting. Betty interrupted their conversation, asking Mrs. Bee if she had seen a little girl around ten years old wearing overalls and a baseball cap. Mrs. Bee mentioned seeing a little boy with overalls and a baseball cap who was with Petey. Betty asked about Petey's whereabouts, and Petey coincidentally entered the front door.

Betty rushed over to Petey to inquire about the little boy he had been with. Petey began sharing details of their encounter, mentioning that the boy talked funny, as if he had a frog in his throat. Betty recognized the description and believed it was Gigi. She pressed further, asking if Petey had seen a colored man with her, but he replied that he hadn't and didn't know which way they had gone. Frustrated, Betty grabbed Mimi, who grabbed a bottle, and they quickly decided to leave. Mr. Willard suggested driving to Alabama to wait for Gigi at her grandmother's house, but Betty had concerns about Bo's involvement.

Mr. Willard revealed that the colored man was Bo, the greatest street fighter of all time. Betty was shocked and recognized the name Bo from her past association with Sophia, an old friend. She didn't realize he was the one who had escaped from prison. Relieved to know Gigi was with him, Betty prayed for their safety and agreed to head to her mother's house in Alabama, hoping no harm would come to Bo. Unbeknownst to them, they had driven past Bo and Gigi after passing the checkpoint.

After a few miles of running and walking in the high bushes, Bo looked out to check if the coast was clear. He then told Gigi to come out from the bushes. They walked along the dirt road until the sun went down. Suddenly, they heard a loud noise. Bo quickly turned around and saw a cloud of dust approaching on the road. He grabbed Gigi and they both jumped into the bushes.

As the noise drew closer, Bo and Gigi peeked out to see what was approaching. It turned out to be Smokey, driving a truck filled with chickens. Bo instructed Gigi to run for the truck. He hopped onto the back of the truck, and with some effort, he managed to pull Gigi up onto it as well.

Smokey said, "I knew we would run into each other again."

Bo replied, "God works in mysterious ways." They both shared a laugh before Bo asked Smokey about the destination of all the chickens. Smokey explained they were headed to his cousin's uncle's niece's house just outside of Alabama, known for making incredible chicken chitlin soup that attracted people from miles around.

Bo and Gigi playfully debated the exact phrasing Smokey used, with Bo insisting it was "uncle's cousin's niece," while Gigi believed it was "cousin's uncle's niece." Smokey stopped the truck and clarified it was "cousin's uncle's niece." They continued their journey, with Bo and Gigi still good-naturedly arguing about it.

Hours passed, and they took turns napping, with Smokey occasionally sipping moonshine to stay alert while singing old country songs. They eventually reached Smokey's destination, where a crowded yard with cars awaited. As the truck stopped, Bo and Gigi peered between the chicken crates to see what was happening.

Music from the jukebox played loudly from the house. Unbeknownst to Bo and Gigi, this was a turning point in their journey. Smokey hopped out of the truck, lit a cigar, and invited them to join him. Bo and Gigi disembarked from the truck.

As they approached the house, five hillbilly boys holding 12-gauge shotguns emerged onto the porch, accompanied by the sheriff. Bo and Gigi halted in their tracks, and more armed men stepped out of parked cars. The sheriff demanded that Bo release the little White girl and they all aimed their guns at him.

Gigi tried to defend Bo, shouting, "He's my friend, he brought no harm to me."

Bowing down on one knee, Bo spoke to Gigi, expressing his lasting memories and words of wisdom.

"I want you to walk up on that porch, don't worry about me. They won't do any harm to me as long as you walk up on that porch," Bo told Gigi, his voice firm but reassuring.

Gigi, terrified for Bo's safety, responded, "Bo, they're aiming to kill you."

"I don't think God is ready for me yet. Now get on, go!"

Gigi reluctantly obeyed, tears streaming down her face as she slowly distanced herself from Bo. Then, a gunshot rang out, hitting Bo in the back. He collapsed to the ground, and Gigi screamed, "No!" before rushing to Bo's side. She tried to rouse him, but he remained unresponsive. Some of the men grabbed Gigi and forcibly pulled her away from Bo, and she fought them off in desperation.

The sheriff approached the person responsible for the accidental shot and demanded an explanation. The man claimed it was an accident, stating that his finger slipped. The sheriff was skeptical and retorted, "Accident, my ass." He ordered the men to load Bo onto the back of his truck.

Smokey's cousin's uncle's niece (clarifying their relation), who was renowned for her chicken chitlin soup, intervened. She offered to tend to Bo and urged the sheriff to let her clean him up. The sheriff, eager for more of her delicious soup, agreed and instructed his men to take Bo into the house. As the sheriff struggled to remember the family relationship, he acknowledged his love for the soup, saying, "I love that damn chicken chitlin soup."

Gigi, meanwhile, was locked in the patrol car. She watched through the rear window, fearing the worst for Bo. In her mind, she believed he was dead, which brought her to tears. Her tears didn't subside, and she cried herself to sleep. It was later revealed that Bo had been shot in the back with rock salt, which had knocked him out and left a painful bruise but ultimately spared his life.

After Smokey's cousin's uncle's niece cleaned up Bo and provided him with a meal, the sheriff promptly handcuffed Bo and placed him in the back of a pick-up truck. With a hint of humor, the sheriff remarked, "Boy, you can't tell me that wasn't the best damn chicken chitlin soup you ever tasted in your life. That damn woman knows how to put her foot in it!"

Bo corrected him, saying, "Sheriff, that's cousin's uncle's niece."

The sheriff, uninterested in the exact relation, retorted, "Cousin's uncle's niece, niece cousin uncle, who gives a shit. That girl can cook. Let's go, boys; we've got a long ride ahead."

Chapter 12

Hours later, Gigi was awakened by her mother, who had arrived to open the back door of the patrol car. Overcome with relief, Betty hugged and kissed her daughter while expressing her gratitude to Jesus for Gigi's safety. Tears welled up in both their eyes as they embraced. Gigi confided in her mother, revealing that her friend Bo had been killed by the "bad men." She believed that if he hadn't been on the train with her, she might have met a worse fate.

With tears in her eyes, Gigi told the sheriff the truth about her adventure on the road with Bo, insisting that he hadn't kidnapped her and had actually saved her life. The sheriff informed her that Bo was alive and had only been shot with rock salt, which had temporarily incapacitated him. He had been transported back to the state prison.

Overjoyed by the news, Gigi jumped up, pleading with her mother to go and get Bo. However, Betty explained that it wouldn't be so simple; Bo had escaped from prison, and although he may not be a bad person, he had broken the law. Gigi was determined to find a way to help him. Betty promised to visit the sheriff's office to inquire about Bo's whereabouts, which earned her daughter's heartfelt gratitude.

The following morning, Gigi and her mother returned to the sheriff's office, where they coincidentally met the sheriff. When Gigi rushed up to him and asked about Bo's prison location, he initially refused to provide the information. Betty joined in, inquiring about the reason behind the secrecy. The sheriff, displaying a hint of racial bias, asked why they were so interested in that "colored boy." Gigi, unable to tolerate the slight against Bo, kicked the sheriff in the leg and defended her friend. The sheriff, annoyed, demanded that they leave and threatened to arrest them for assault. Gigi's face turned red with anger, and Betty decided it was time to find another way to locate Bo.

Bo, on the other hand, had been transferred to the Eastern State Penitentiary in Philadelphia. His sentence was fifteen years of hard labor. Despite the ugly bruise on his back from the rock salt shot, it hadn't slowed him down.

Days turned into weeks, and weeks turned into months. Bo endured his daily toil, breaking rocks with a sledgehammer and clearing long stretches of weeds, undeterred by the arduous labor and harsh conditions. He wore a constant smile, refusing to let anything or anyone break his spirit. Meanwhile, Gigi's daily routine consisted of running to the coffee shop after school, hoping to receive news of Bo's whereabouts. However, her mother's response remained consistent each day: no information yet.

To brighten Gigi's spirits, Betty treated her to her favorite vanilla milkshake, which worked like a charm, transforming her frown into a radiant smile. Betty couldn't help but express her love for her daughter, stating, "That's my little angel."

While sipping her milkshake, Gigi was suddenly struck by an idea. Excitedly, she approached her mother, exclaiming, "Mama, I just thought of something. Can you get the names and addresses of the penitentiaries in the South? I will write letters to Bo and send one to every one of them." Betty enthusiastically agreed, promising to visit the post office during her break the following day. Gigi felt an overwhelming sense of hope and eagerly anticipated the next day.

With time passing, Gigi diligently composed letters addressed to every Southern penitentiary. She checked the mailbox daily in anticipation of a response from Bo. Her mother, however, offered words of comfort, urging her to be patient, as life's surprises often come when least expected.

Then one day, Betty suddenly dropped to her knees, gripped by a violent fit of coughing and clutching her stomach. Concerned, Gigi rushed to her mother's side, asking what was wrong. Betty, struggling to catch her breath, extended her hand to keep Gigi away and reassured her that she would recover on her own. Gigi retrieved a towel and handed it to her mother, who wiped her face and coughed into it.

Returning to the house, Betty sat down on the couch, feeling lightheaded. Gigi offered to wipe her mother's forehead with the towel. To her shock, the towel was stained with blood. Gigi, understanding the gravity of the situation, began to cry as she realized that her mother was seriously ill. Despite her tears, she managed to fetch another towel for her mother. Betty then asked for a cigarette, and Gigi, pretending to check the empty box, was relieved to find none left. She gave her mother the box and wiped her brow.

Gigi considered fetching Dr. Johnson, but her mother declined, insisting she would be fine. Eventually, Betty fell asleep, and Gigi, determined to watch over her, stayed by her side throughout the night. Fatigue eventually overcame Gigi, and she drifted off to sleep in the front room, still keeping a close watch on her ailing mother.

As time went by, Gigi maintained her daily routine after school, heading straight to the coffee shop. However, when she walked in one day, an unusual atmosphere hung in the air. The regular patrons all wore somber expressions, heads hanging low. Gigi, sensing something was amiss, asked, "What's going on? Why is everyone so down? Where's my mom?"

Mr. Willard beckoned her over. "Gigi, come over here, I need to talk to you."

Anxious and worried, Gigi demanded to know her mother's whereabouts and began calling out for her frantically. Tears welled up in her eyes.

Mr. Willard approached Gigi and gently explained, "Your mom is in the hospital. She passed out on the floor. Come on, I'll take you to see your mom."

They hurried to the hospital, where Gigi learned her mother's room number and rushed inside. She found Betty standing by the window, smoking a cigarette, which she quickly extinguished upon seeing her daughter's arrival.

Gigi ran to her mother, embracing her tightly.

"How's my little angel? Mommy's okay, I just lost my balance, that's all. I'll be out of here in a few days."

However, Gigi, perceptive beyond her years, acknowledged the truth. "Mama, I'm not dumb. I know you have cancer."

"Yeah, you're right, I do."

"Can they get rid of it?"

"They're doing the best they can, but I'm not going anywhere until I see you graduate from high school."

Gigi, after a pause, questioned what would happen after her graduation, to which Betty had no clear answer, simply holding her daughter close and expressing her love.

After a few weeks, Betty was discharged from the hospital, although she couldn't return to work. To support her and her mother, Gigi took on a part-time job delivering food for Mr. Willard. After her shifts, she would bike back home to care for her ailing mother. The town doctor made regular visits to check on Betty's condition, and the kind-hearted townspeople extended their support by providing food and assisting with household chores.

Antoinette, Gigi's best friend, despite her aversion to getting dirty, played her part in helping Gigi with tasks such as washing pigs on hot days. As time flew by, Gigi and Antoinette successfully graduated from high school. Throughout this period, Betty's health remained fragile, her memory coming and going. Attempts to have her readmitted to the hospital were met with resistance, as she refused to return.

Antoinette decided to attend college, but Gigi took on the role of manager at the coffee shop. Meanwhile, Mr. Willard's health declined due to arthritis in his legs, rendering him unable to work.

Bo was no longer toiling in the fields due to his age, and he never received any communication from his family during his prison sentence, leaving him unsure about who was still alive or who had passed away.

CHAPTER 13

Fifteen years had passed, and Gigi was now twenty-five years old. Mr. Willard, the owner of the coffee shop, informed Gigi that she was to become the new boss as he was retiring. After her shifts, Gigi would return home to care for her mother.

One day around noon, a man of color entered the coffee shop and took a seat at one of the tables. Ms. Knight, one of the waitresses, approached him. "What can I get you?"

The man requested a cup of coffee and a slice of apple pie from the counter.

"Coming right up."

Gigi, who was busy at the cash register, noticed the man sitting in the corner. She couldn't help but think, *I've never seen him in here before.* The man, sporting a gray beard and

gray hair on his head, caught her attention, and she found herself staring at him.

When the man had finished his coffee and pie, he walked over to the cash register, and Gigi asked him, "The waitress didn't give you a receipt?"

"No."

Gigi raised her voice, calling out to Ms. Knight, and asked her why she hadn't provided the man with a receipt.

Ms. Knight, nonchalantly chewing gum, responded, "I forgot."

Gigi, feeling a sense of frustration, remarked, "I can't depend on anybody around here."

The man retorted, "If you can't depend on yourself, how are you going to depend on anybody else? Remember that." He then handed Gigi the money for the pie and coffee, turned around, and walked out of the coffee shop.

Gigi stood there deep in thought, and suddenly, it struck her. The man's words were just like what Bo had told her when she was ten years old. Gigi dropped the money on the floor, rushed out into the street, and didn't spot the man anywhere. She called out, "Mister, come back! Where are you?" The commotion drew the attention of the townspeople, who started coming outside to see what was happening.

Meanwhile, the man had emerged from behind a building and stood in the middle of the street. As Gigi approached him, she asked, "Your name wouldn't happen to be Bo, would it?"

The man took off his cap. "Your name wouldn't happen to be Miss Gigi, would it?"

Gigi beamed with a big smile and embraced Bo. "It's really you."

"Ask Smokey's cousin's uncle's niece," he said, which made Gigi burst into laughter.

EPILOGUE

Michael expressed his amazement, saying, "Wow, Grandma, that was an amazing story."

Gigi responded, "Yep, yep, yep, yep, yep. It's past my suppertime; let's go into the house."

They made their way toward the front house, but a man was standing by the front door.

"Grandma, who's that man at your door?"

"Probably them damn Jehovah Witness people again. I gave them some money two days ago."

Gigi yelled out to the man at her front door, "I don't need no more magazines, and I just gave y'all money two days ago."

The man turned around. "Excuse me."

"Oh, you're not one of them, are you? Why are you at my door?"

"My name is Bo Junior. I'm looking for a lady by the name of Gigi. I was told she knew a lot about my father, Bo Senior."

Gigi responded with a display of excitement, laughing and exclaiming, "Kick me twice, then over the moon! I can't believe my eyes. I see you took after your mama."

"Yes, I guess I did."

Michael, perplexed, asked Gigi, "Grandma, what do you mean he took after his mama?"

"Like you, Michael. You took after your punk ass daddy. He used to get beat up after school, too."

Bo Junior burst into laughter and, addressing Michael, explained, "Your grandma, Gigi, was talking about my skin color. My mom was white, and my father, Bo, was dark brown."

Michael understood and said, "Oh."

Gigi took Bo Junior's hand, and the three of them walked to the back house. Gigi began sharing stories with Bo Junior about his father.

Michael, somewhat resigned, commented, "Here we go again."

THE END.

Embarking on a journey that led him to the heart of Los Angeles, Darryl Barnes found himself standing amidst the towering structures of Fifth Street, a surreal echo of the very dreams that had haunted his subconscious. Unbeknownst to him, this urban landscape, reminiscent of his visions, would be the canvas upon which his remarkable transformation unfolded.

As fate would have it, the cab's drop-off point marked the intersection between destitution and opportunity for Darryl. Amidst the shadows of homelessness, he became a beacon of resilience, attracting the attention of those willing to extend a lifeline. A job offer and a dignified place to call home materialized, rescuing him from the clutches of hellish despair.

Darryl Barnes, once ensnared by the walls of adversity, emerged as an exemplar of the profound wisdom articulated by Dr. Rosie Milligan: "Where you are today is no reflection of your tomorrow." In the vibrant tapestry of Los Angeles, Darryl not only transcended his past but blossomed into an outstanding and industrious resident.

In 2014, Darryl penned his autobiography, *The Book of D. Barnes: As I Walked Through The Streets of Los Angeles,*

Homelessness Was The Springboard to My Destiny. Undeterred by life's trials, he now ventures into uncharted literary territory with his latest creation, *Tomboy Gigi and the Fugitive.* This novel promises to grip your emotions relentlessly, holding you hostage from the opening chapter to the very last page.

Darryl Barnes, a testament to the indomitable human spirit, continues to craft narratives that resonate with the power of resilience and the promise of a brighter tomorrow.